The Prince Consort

Prince Albert at the Age of Twenty-four
Miniature by Robert Thorburn (Royal Collection)

The Queen's favourite portrait of Prince Albert, Thorburn's miniature, now badly cracked, depicts him in medieval armour to gratify a wish often expressed by Queen Victoria. The picture was a birthday present from the Prince to the Queen on 24 May 1844, and as late as 20 December 1873 the Queen wrote, 'This portrait gives the Prince's real expression more than anything she [the Queen] knows. During the fatal illness, and on the last morning of his life, he was wonderfully like this picture.'

THE WORLD
AND THE AGE
OF PRINCE ALBERT

The Prince Consort
MAN OF MANY FACETS

GODFREY
&
MARGARET SCHEELE

ORESKO BOOKS LTD · LONDON

Acknowledgements

We would like to express our grateful appreciation to all those whose assistance and advice have made this book possible, in the first place to Her Majesty the Queen by whose gracious permission we have been able to work in the Royal Library at Windsor Castle and to reproduce pictures from the Royal Collections. In this connection we are particularly indebted to the Librarian, Sir Robert Mackworth-Young, the Hon. Mrs. Jane Roberts and the staff of the Royal Library and also to Sir Oliver Millar, Surveyor of the Queen's Pictures and his staff. Our gratitude is due also to the Factor of Balmoral, Col. W. G. McHardy.

We would like to thank many of our former colleagues in the British Museum and British Library for the unfailing kindness, facilities and advice extended to us. Our special thanks are due to the Keeper of the Department of Prints and Drawings and his staff, particularly Mr. Reginald Williams and Mr. Peter Moore, as also to Mr. Edward Croft-Murray, the late Keeper of that Department; to the Keeper and staff of the Department of Coins and Medals and especially to Mrs. Joan Martin. We are most grateful to Dr. Richnall and the authorities and staff of the British Library for the facilities offered to us and particularly to Dr. Helen Wallis, Mr. Ernest Jones and the staff of the Map Room, and to Mr. A. H. King and the staff of the Music Room.

We are most appreciative of the facilities and rights of reproduction afforded to us at the National Gallery, the National Portrait Gallery and the Victoria and Albert Museum. We are most indebted to Dr. Friedrich Karl von Siebold of Munich who very kindly allowed us to reproduce the portrait of Dr. Charlotte von Siebold. We would like to acknowledge also the facilities afforded by the London Library, the Oxted Public Library, the library of the Royal Institute of International Affairs and the Wiener Library and the assistance of the staff of those bodies. We would also like to express our appreciation and thanks to our publisher, Mr. Robert Oresko and his staff.

Godfrey and Margaret Scheele
Limpsfield, August 1976

First published in Great Britain by
Oresko Books Ltd., 30 Notting Hill Gate, London W11

UK ISBN 0 905368 06 1 (cloth)
UK ISBN 0 905368 07 X (paper)

Copyright © Oresko Books Ltd. 1977

Printed in Great Britain by
Burgess & Son (Abingdon) Ltd., Abingdon, Oxfordshire

Library of Congress Cataloging in Publication Data

Scheele, Godfrey.
    The Prince Consort.

    (Oresko art book series)
    Bibliography: p.
    1. Albert, Consort of Queen Victoria, 1819-1861.
    2. Great Britain—Princes and princesses—Biography.
    3. Great Britain—History—Victoria, 1837-1901.
I. Scheele, Margaret, joint author. II. Title.
    III. Series.
    DA559.A1.S33   941.081'092'4. (B)   77-70921.
    USA ISBN 0-8467-0321-1
    USA ISBN 0-8467-0322-X pbk.

Contents

Preface	7
Genealogies	8
The First Coburg Marriage: Leopold and Charlotte	13
The Second Coburg Marriage: the Duke and Duchess of Kent	21
Albert of Saxe-Coburg: the Grooming Years	31
Albert and Victoria: the Golden Years	51
'Those two Dreadful Old Men' and the Great Exhibition	81
The Crimean War, the French Alliance and Balmoral	95
The Prussian Marriage: Prince Albert's German Dream	113
The Tragic Dénouement: 1861	125
Bibliography	133

Preface

This book does not attempt to provide a new biography of the Prince Consort. It seeks rather to depict him, a man of many facets, in the geographical and historical setting in which he lived and pursued his manifold interests, royal and domestic, political and diplomatic, artistic and musical.

The story is initiated by the tragic idyll of Leopold and Charlotte which both set the scene and determined the development of the story of Albert and Victoria. Leopold and Albert were 'alike in many ways and yet so different', wrote the Queen's half-sister Feodora. It was Leopold's influence, based on his experience, which was to guide so strongly both his nephew and his niece.

In Belgium Leopold made the monarchy respectable according to the new middle-class standards, and Albert with Victoria gave the stamp of this new model monarchy to that of England. It was to be a monarchy of peace because Albert was a man of peace. Germany was the focus of Albert's dreams, but England reflected his creation.

The character and personality of Prince Albert can only be understood against the background of his age and nation. Albert was a German of the generation which spanned the period between the cultural efflorescence of Goethe and Schiller and the iron age of Bismarck which purported to realize its ideals. Albert was born in 1819; the generation of his father and uncle had participated in the epic War of Liberation against Napoleon. National unity and constitutional liberty were the goals deriving from Schiller's dramas which these men sought and felt cheated of. With all their habitual idealism, the young Germans of Albert's generation were gripped with this same enthusiasm. Leopold and Stockmar, Albert and his brother Ernest, Charles of Leiningen and Christian Bunsen, professors and business men, all in varying degrees were caught up in the maelstrom of the movement for German unity, which found expression in the Frankfurt Parliament of 1848, but realization only in the debased alloy of Bismarck's Empire in 1871.

England and her literature had been an inspiration for Lessing, Goethe and Schiller, her Protestantism and her Constitution appealed to Germany's Liberals. Albert felt himself, married to the Queen of England, father of the prospective Queen of Prussia, to be playing a vocational rôle in the achievement of Germany's destiny in close alliance with England.

The world of Albert and Victoria was born out of the ashes of 1789, and it vanished in the holocaust of 1914. The ideals for which Albert strove have only come to realization a century later in the German Federal Republic of Adenauer, Heuss and Schmidt, firmly set like Great Britain in the European Community, as a bulwark now, as then, against the threat of Russian aggression.

THE ENGLISH ROYAL HOUSE 1760—1901

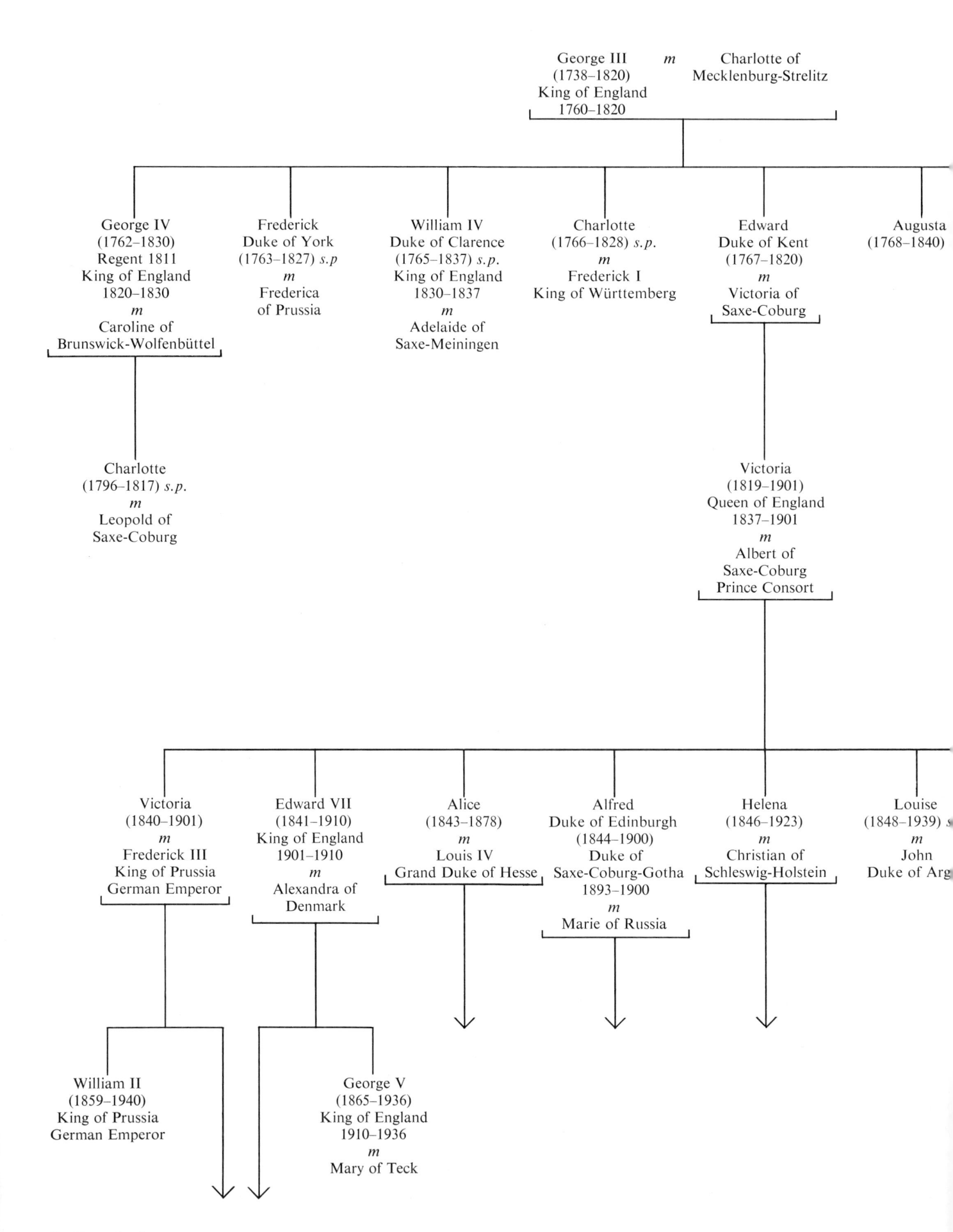

```
George III  m  Charlotte of
(1738–1820)    Mecklenburg-Strelitz
King of England
1760–1820
```

Children of George III and Charlotte:

- **George IV** (1762–1830), Regent 1811, King of England 1820–1830, m Caroline of Brunswick-Wolfenbüttel
  - **Charlotte** (1796–1817) s.p., m Leopold of Saxe-Coburg
- **Frederick Duke of York** (1763–1827) s.p, m Frederica of Prussia
- **William IV Duke of Clarence** (1765–1837) s.p., King of England 1830–1837, m Adelaide of Saxe-Meiningen
- **Charlotte** (1766–1828) s.p., m Frederick I King of Württemberg
- **Edward Duke of Kent** (1767–1820), m Victoria of Saxe-Coburg
  - **Victoria** (1819–1901), Queen of England 1837–1901, m Albert of Saxe-Coburg, Prince Consort
- **Augusta** (1768–1840)

Children of Victoria and Albert:

- **Victoria** (1840–1901), m Frederick III King of Prussia, German Emperor
  - **William II** (1859–1940), King of Prussia, German Emperor →
- **Edward VII** (1841–1910), King of England 1901–1910, m Alexandra of Denmark
  - **George V** (1865–1936), King of England 1910–1936, m Mary of Teck →
- **Alice** (1843–1878), m Louis IV Grand Duke of Hesse ↓
- **Alfred Duke of Edinburgh** (1844–1900), Duke of Saxe-Coburg-Gotha 1893–1900, m Marie of Russia ↓
- **Helena** (1846–1923), m Christian of Schleswig-Holstein ↓
- **Louise** (1848–1939) s, m John Duke of Arg[yll]

8 Genealogies

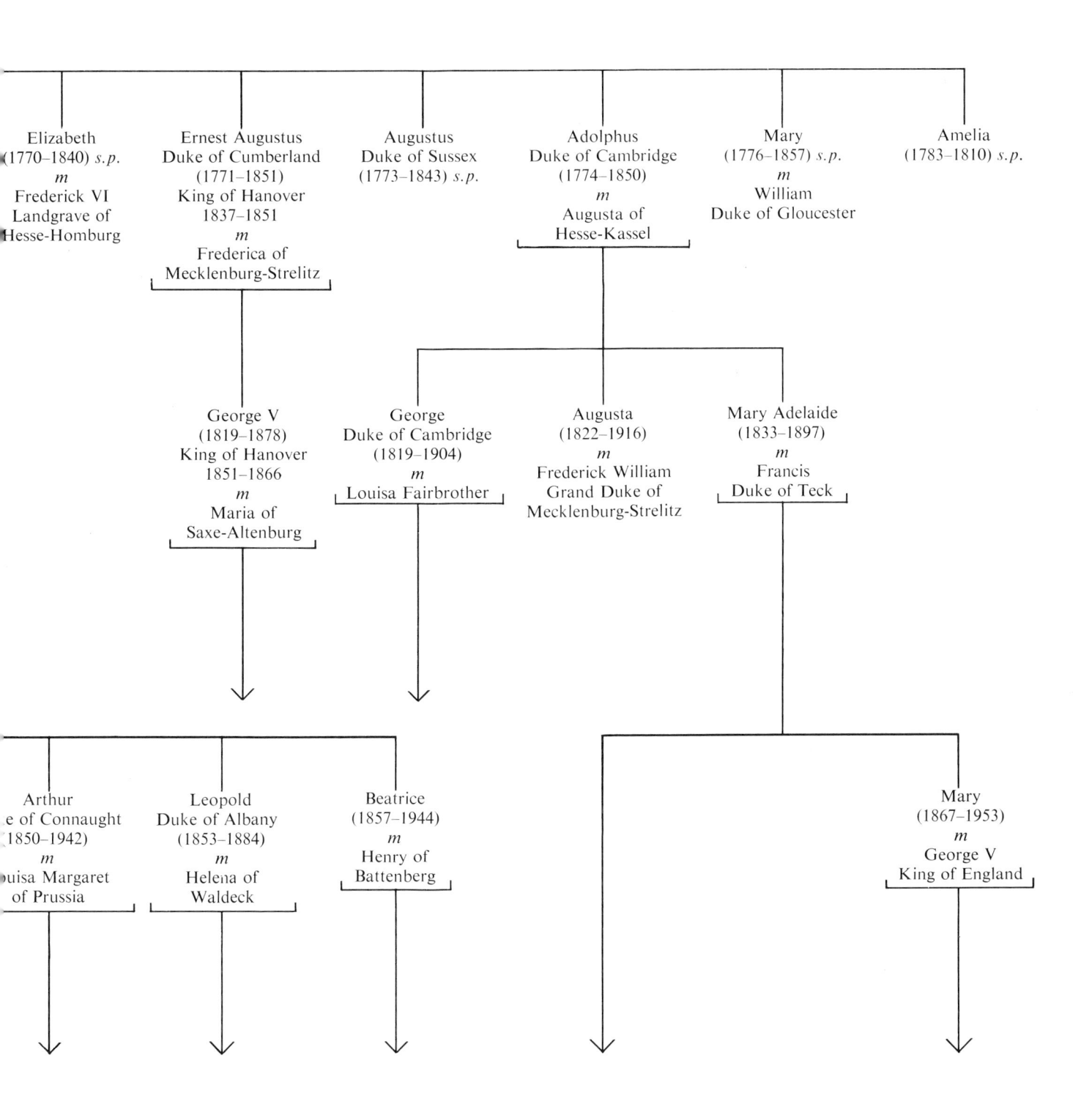

```
┌──────────────┬──────────────┬──────────────┬──────────────┬──────────────┬──────────────┐
│              │              │              │              │              │              │
Elizabeth    Ernest Augustus  Augustus      Adolphus         Mary          Amelia
(1770–1840) s.p. Duke of Cumberland Duke of Sussex Duke of Cambridge (1776–1857) s.p. (1783–1810) s.p.
m            (1771–1851)     (1773–1843) s.p. (1774–1850)      m
Frederick VI  King of Hanover                  m              William
Landgrave of  1837–1851                      Augusta of      Duke of Gloucester
Hesse-Homburg    m                          Hesse-Kassel
             Frederica of
             Mecklenburg-Strelitz
```

- George V (1819–1878) King of Hanover 1851–1866 m Maria of Saxe-Altenburg
- George Duke of Cambridge (1819–1904) m Louisa Fairbrother
- Augusta (1822–1916) m Frederick William Grand Duke of Mecklenburg-Strelitz
- Mary Adelaide (1833–1897) m Francis Duke of Teck

- Arthur e of Connaught (1850–1942) m Louisa Margaret of Prussia
- Leopold Duke of Albany (1853–1884) m Helena of Waldeck
- Beatrice (1857–1944) m Henry of Battenberg
- Mary (1867–1953) m George V King of England

Genealogies 9

THE HOUSE OF SAXE-COBURG-GOTHA IN GERMANY AND EUROPE

(*Members of the House of Orléans are in italics*)

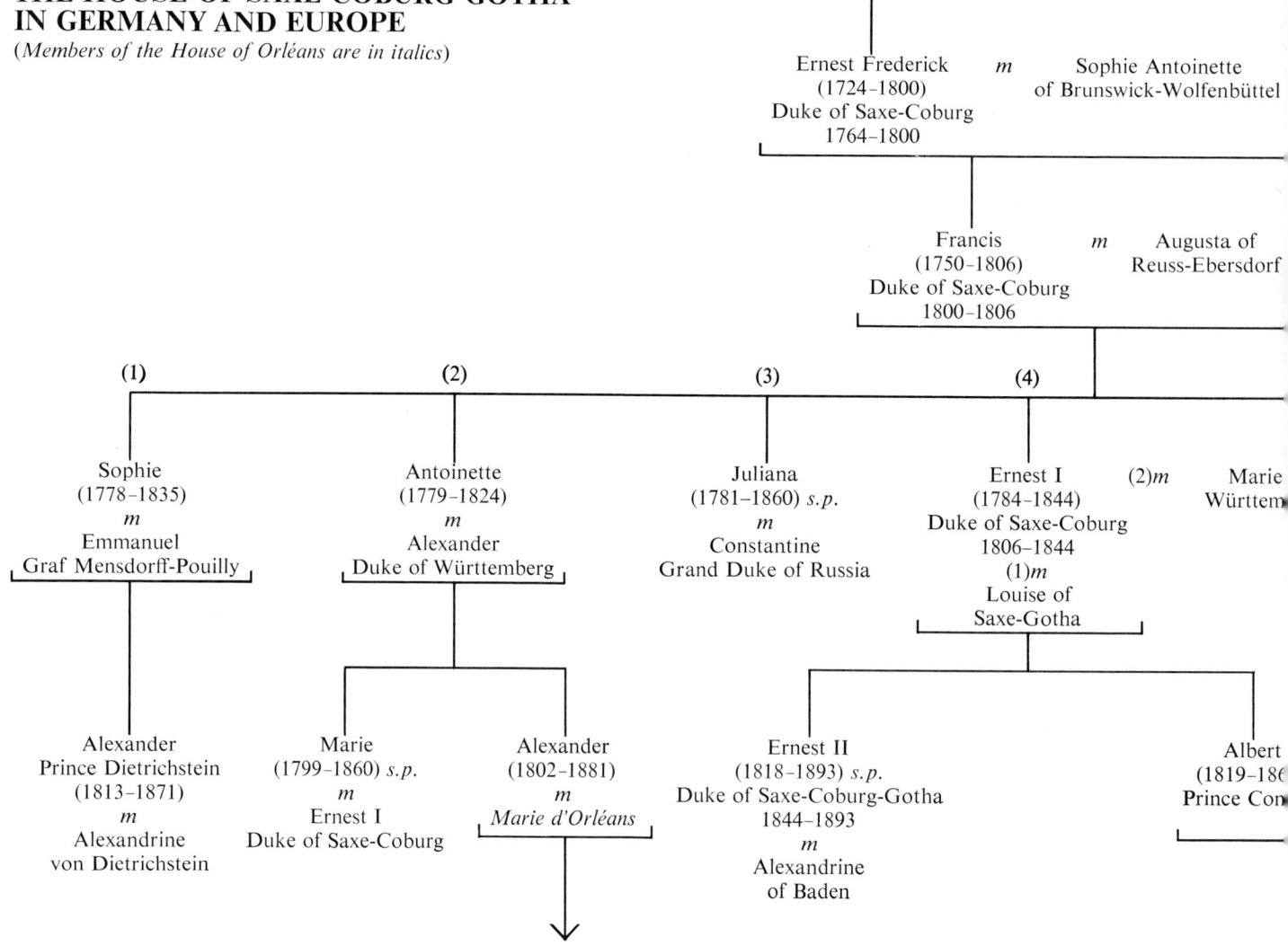

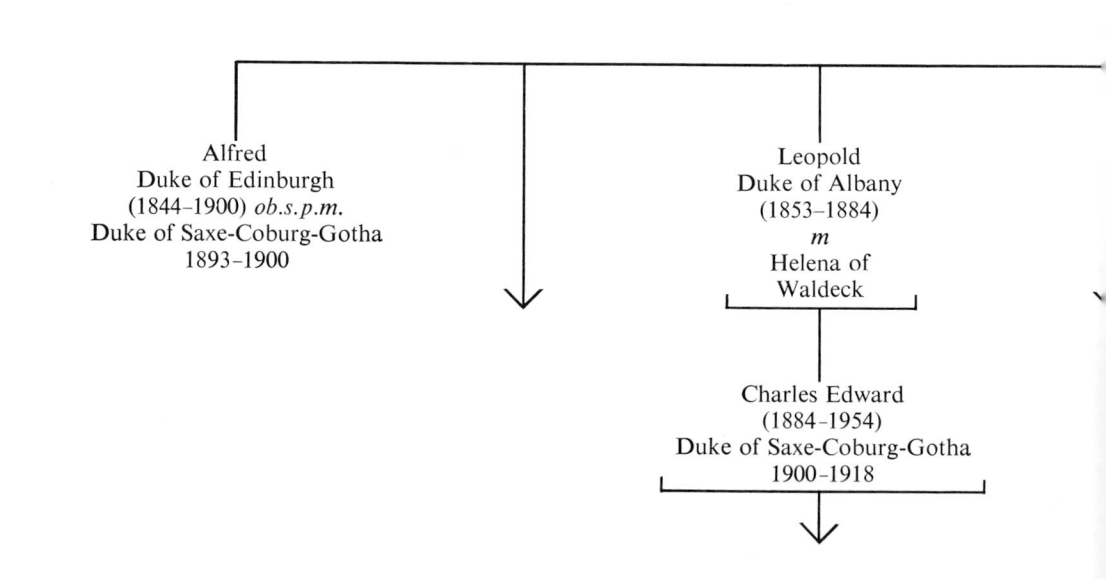

```
Ernest Frederick          m    Sophie Antoinette
(1724-1800)                    of Brunswick-Wolfenbüttel
Duke of Saxe-Coburg
1764-1800
            │
        Francis            m    Augusta of
        (1750-1806)             Reuss-Ebersdorf
        Duke of Saxe-Coburg
        1800-1806
```

(1) Sophie (1778-1835) m Emmanuel Graf Mensdorff-Pouilly
— Alexander Prince Dietrichstein (1813-1871) m Alexandrine von Dietrichstein

(2) Antoinette (1779-1824) m Alexander Duke of Württemberg
— Marie (1799-1860) *s.p.* m Ernest I Duke of Saxe-Coburg
— Alexander (1802-1881) m *Marie d'Orléans* ↓

(3) Juliana (1781-1860) *s.p.* m Constantine Grand Duke of Russia

(4) Ernest I (1784-1844) Duke of Saxe-Coburg 1806-1844
   (2) m Marie Württem…
   (1) m Louise of Saxe-Gotha
— Ernest II (1818-1893) *s.p.* Duke of Saxe-Coburg-Gotha 1844-1893 m Alexandrine of Baden
— Albert (1819-186…) Prince Con…

— Alfred Duke of Edinburgh (1844-1900) *ob.s.p.m.* Duke of Saxe-Coburg-Gotha 1893-1900
— Leopold Duke of Albany (1853-1884) m Helena of Waldeck
   — Charles Edward (1884-1954) Duke of Saxe-Coburg-Gotha 1900-1918 ↓

10 Genealogies

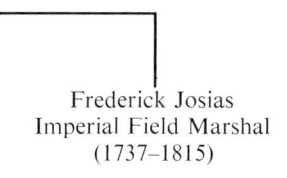

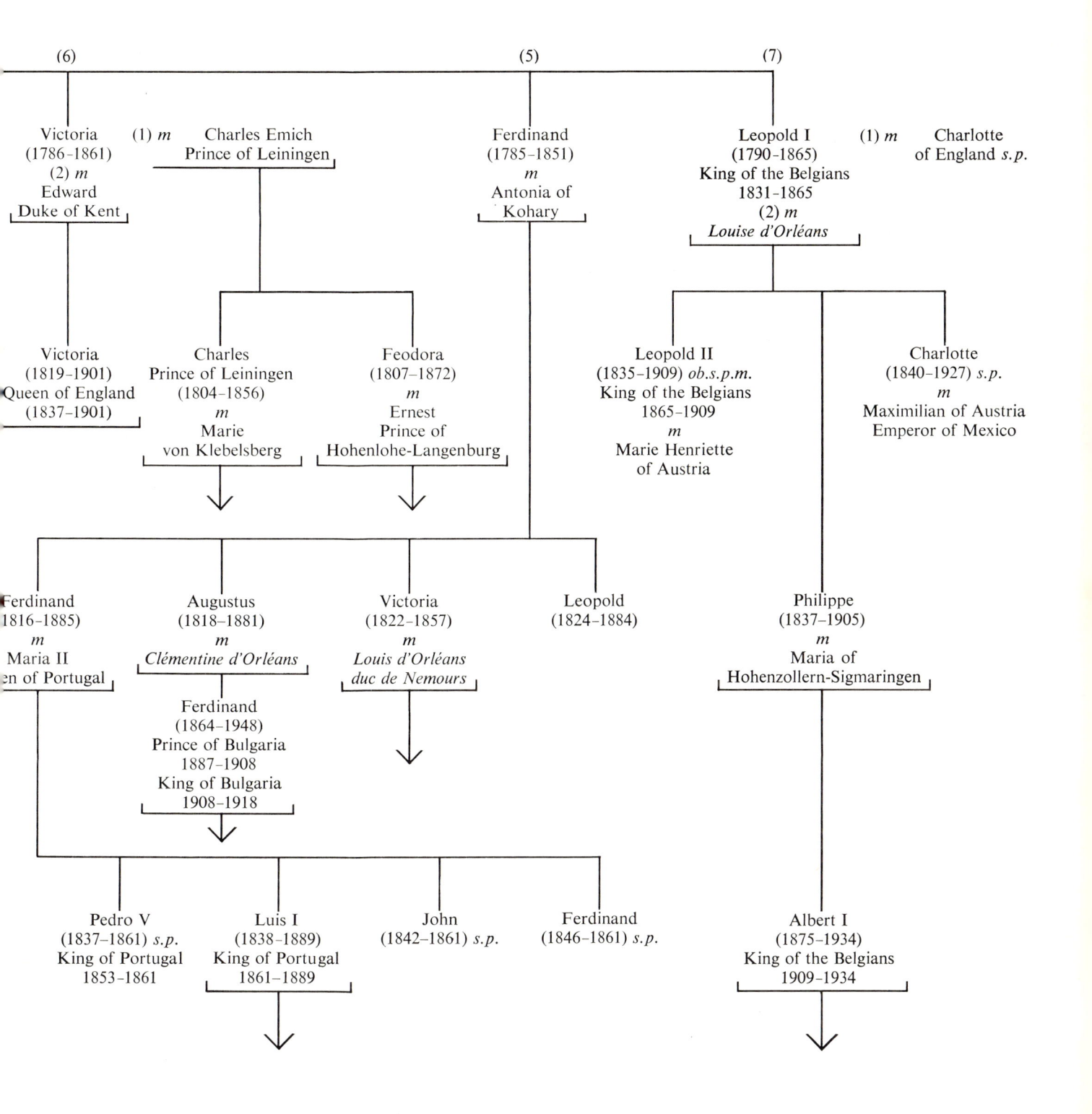

Frederick Josias
Imperial Field Marshal
(1737–1815)

(6) | (5) | (7)

Victoria (1786–1861) (1) m Charles Emich Prince of Leiningen
(2) m Edward Duke of Kent

Ferdinand (1785–1851) m Antonia of Kohary

Leopold I (1790–1865) King of the Belgians 1831–1865 (1) m Charlotte of England s.p.
(2) m *Louise d'Orléans*

Victoria (1819–1901) Queen of England (1837–1901)

Charles Prince of Leiningen (1804–1856) m Marie von Klebelsberg ↓

Feodora (1807–1872) m Ernest Prince of Hohenlohe-Langenburg ↓

Leopold II (1835–1909) *ob.s.p.m.* King of the Belgians 1865–1909 m Marie Henriette of Austria

Charlotte (1840–1927) s.p. m Maximilian of Austria Emperor of Mexico

Ferdinand (1816–1885) m Maria II en of Portugal

Augustus (1818–1881) m *Clémentine d'Orléans*
Ferdinand (1864–1948) Prince of Bulgaria 1887–1908 King of Bulgaria 1908–1918 ↓

Victoria (1822–1857) m *Louis d'Orléans duc de Nemours* ↓

Leopold (1824–1884)

Philippe (1837–1905) m Maria of Hohenzollern-Sigmaringen

Pedro V (1837–1861) s.p. King of Portugal 1853–1861

Luis I (1838–1889) King of Portugal 1861–1889 ↓

John (1842–1861) s.p.

Ferdinand (1846–1861) s.p.

Albert I (1875–1934) King of the Belgians 1909–1934 ↓

Genealogies 11

Prince Leopold of Saxe-Coburg, later Leopold I, King of the Belgians (1790–1865)
Engraving by F. C. Lewis after a drawing by Sir George Hayter. Published 1 August 1816 (British Museum)

The First Coburg Marriage: Leopold and Charlotte

In June 1814 London, capital of the power which had fought Napoleon longest, welcomed in the hour of victory the Allied sovereigns of Prussia and Russia. The rôle of host was played by the Prince of Wales as Regent for his blind father King George III. There was no hostess because the Prince had separated from his wife immediately after the birth of their only child, Princess Charlotte, then aged eighteen. After a most unhappy childhood, due to her parents' dissensions, she had accepted as a means of escape engagement to the Prince of Orange, heir to the kingdom of the Netherlands.

Such an alliance ran counter to Russian policy, however, and so the Tsar sent his sister to London, where she became a close confidante of Princess Charlotte and introduced to her a handsome young major-general of the Tsar's suite, Prince Leopold of Saxe-Coburg, member of an impoverished but well-connected German family. Charlotte now broke off her engagement, to the fury of her father, who kept her isolated in Windsor Forest, but thanks to her favourite uncle, Edward, Duke of Kent, she was able to correspond with Leopold, who was successfully exercising his diplomatic skill at the Congress of Vienna.

In February 1816 Leopold returned to Britain at the invitation of the Prince Regent, and on 2 May he and Charlotte were married. Parliament granted him an annual allowance of £50,000 for life, and Marlborough House became their residence in London, where they were greeted enthusiastically everywhere. But they were happiest in their country home, Claremont House near Esher, where they could enjoy their garden, music, reading and above all each other, despite the profound differences in their characters, for she was impetuous and outspoken, while he measured every word carefully. Leopold had brought from Coburg as his personal physician Christian Stockmar, who was to play a key rôle in English royal history over the next generation. Charlotte found in 'Stocky' an agreeable companion, especially when Leopold's ponderous seriousness became excessive.

On 5 November 1817 Charlotte gave birth to a stillborn son and died herself the next day. It was a tragic day for Britain, for the Royal Family and above all for Leopold. Stockmar often said, 'The Princess had not died so young and so sore a death, if I had treated her by myself in the German way.' Stockmar's advice had not been sought, but the memory of Charlotte's death in childbirth was to haunt England's Royal Family.

Leopold's mother, the Dowager Duchess Augusta of Coburg, who had never met Charlotte, wrote in her diary, 'She is dead, that beautiful, charming, good woman, the hope of a great people she was to reign over; and whose death has ruined the happiness of poor Leopold's life. God's ways are mysterious, often terrible. No mortal can understand why this lovely flower had to fade in the morning of her life, and without the fruit with which she would have blessed her country.'

Prince Leopold of Saxe-Coburg, later Leopold I, King of the Belgians (1790–1865)
Anonymous miniature (Royal Collection)

Leopold was the youngest and most able son of Francis, Duke of Saxe-Coburg and Augusta of Reuss-Ebersdorf. In the hour of supreme adversity after Napoleon's victory over Prussia at Jena in 1806 and following his father's death, he was his mother's main support, together with his great-uncle Prince Frederick Josias. Thanks to the latter's military prowess, Prince Leopold had the Emperor Leopold II as his godfather. His sister's marriage to a Russian grand duke, albeit most unhappy, secured him early advancement in the Russian Army, and he claimed to have been the first German prince to join it in 1813. Napoleon described him as 'the handsomest young man I ever saw at the Tuileries', and his comeliness gained him the favour of the Empress Josephine and her daughter Queen Hortense. In London in 1814 Leopold quickly won the heart of Princess Charlotte and made friends with the Dukes of York and Kent as with Castlereagh and Wellington, while at the Congress of Vienna his diplomatic skill gained the Rhenish principality of Lichtenberg for Coburg. In Vienna he was also one of the most admired of the twenty-four champions in a knightly tournament popular in the Romantic age of Walter Scott.

In 1816 the Prince Regent consented to his marriage to Princess Charlotte, but the future George IV never liked his son-in-law, calling him 'Marquis Peu-à-peu' and 'Monsieur Tout-doucement' in reference to his caution and care in weighing every word and action. After Charlotte's premature death Leopold decided, on the advice of his secretary Stockmar, to stay in England where a new rôle fell to him as financial and moral support to his sister the Duchess of Kent and her daughter Victoria. 'Uncle Leopold' and Claremont played a considerable rôle in the future Queen's childhood and youth. It was also at this time that Leopold was attracted to Stockmar's cousin, the actress Caroline Bauer, who bore a remarkable physical resemblance to Princess Charlotte and whom he installed in a house in Regent's Park.

(*opposite*)
Prince Frederick Josias of Saxe-Coburg-Saalfeld (1737–1815)
Engraving by C. Müller after a painting by F. Jagemann (British Museum)

Prince Frederick Josias stands at the fountainhead of the story of Leopold and Albert of Saxe-Coburg. The introduction of primogeniture in Coburg in 1747 obliged him, as a younger son, to seek his fortune in the Austrian Army, where he had a distinguished career and became the last Field Marshal of the Holy Roman Empire. After his unsuccessful campaign in the southern Netherlands against the French Revolutionary armies he retired to Coburg where he became the focal figure of the ducal family and the pride of the populace, participating in their shooting competitions, often as the victorious 'Schützenkönig', until his seventy-seventh year. In 1806 it was his intervention which mitigated the severities of French occupation.

Duchess Augusta wrote on his death, 'His character was such a truly noble one and so full of real sympathy. Few people play their part in life so well up to the very end, as he did without any lapse or weakness. In his youth he was a good son and enjoyed to the full a happy guileless life. Later on he became a very distinguished soldier and a good leader, the pride of his whole family, who probably without him would never have taken such a prominent part in the annals of the times. In his old age he was a calm and happy man and kind to everyone. Till the last months of his life he had never been ill, therefore pain to which he was unaccustomed, struck him harder than other people, but his brain remained clear and bright until the last.'

His great-nephew Prince Leopold was his particular favourite because of his intellectual and physical gifts and he encouraged him in his ambitions and career. Leopold's letters from Paris to his great-uncle gave fine descriptions of persons and conditions there. The artist's father had been librarian to the Dowager Duchess Anna Amalia of Saxe-Weimar and his sister Caroline Jagemann, the well-known actress, became the mistress of Goethe's patron, Karl August, Duke of Saxe-Weimar.

14 Leopold and Charlotte

Friedrich Josias
Prinz zu Sachsen Coburg &c.
Kaiserl. Königl. Feldmarschall.

Seiner Herzogl. Durchlaucht Herrn Ernst, regierendem Herzoge zu Sachsen Coburg und Saalfeld &c.

Leopold and Charlotte 15

Princess Charlotte of Wales (1796–1817)
Painting by George Dawe (National Portrait Gallery)

In 1795 George, Prince of Wales was married to his cousin Caroline of Brunswick-Wolfenbüttel in order to assure the succession to the British crown. From the first the marriage was unhappy, and the two partners developed increasing bitterness and enmity towards each other. The only issue was Princess Charlotte, whose childhood and youth were ruined by her parents' disputes. She often told Christian Stockmar 'My mother was bad, but she would not have been so bad if my father had not been much worse still.' The first enduring happiness in her life came with her marriage to Leopold of Saxe-Coburg in May 1816. She called herself the happiest woman in the land, and Stockmar said the greatness of her love for Leopold was only to be compared with the National Debt.

Her life at Claremont brought out Charlotte's best qualities, her personal kindness and generosity and a majestic dignity. 'Her dress was always extremely neat and well-chosen, but was in no way distinguished from that of any lady living in the country, except insofar as her truly royal deportment might set it off. The same order and punctuality which she observed in her attire she carried into everything she did. Her letters were models of clearness and definiteness,' wrote a contemporary English biographer. Her death was a terrible blow to Leopold, who claimed never to have recovered the happiness of his short life with Charlotte. 'It is perhaps the strongest of all testimonies to the worth of the Princess Charlotte that she should have inspired a man by nature so cautious and reserved with an attachment not less passionate than her own,' said Lady Rose Weigall.

Claremont House, the south front
Engraving by D. Havell after a painting by J. Hassell (British Library)

A mansion was originally built on this site by Vanbrugh for the Duke of Newcastle, but when Robert Clive of India purchased the estate in 1768 he commissioned 'Capability' Brown to erect a new Palladian residence and to redesign the grounds. A million and a half bricks were made in the park, and the house with its four façades was built, regardless of cost and according to Brown's plans, by his son-in-law, Henry Holland. According to Macaulay the locals believed the 'wicked Lord had ordered the walls to be made so thick in order to keep out the Devil.' It is doubtful if Clive ever lived there. In 1816 the house was purchased for Princess Charlotte and her husband, who spent there the happiest months of her short life and his long one. She died at Claremont House after giving birth to a stillborn son.

Prince Leopold retained the residence and it provided a welcome change from London for Princess Victoria, who later renewed her happy childhood memories by often bringing Prince Albert and their older children there. She wrote to her uncle (10 January 1843), 'This place has a peculiar charm for us both and to me it brings back recollections of the happiest days of my otherwise dull childhood, when I experienced such kindness from you, dearest Uncle, kindness which has ever since continued.' In 1848 King Leopold lent it as a refuge to his father-in-law Louis Philippe, King of the French. The Orléans family resided at Claremont throughout the Second Empire in France until 1866. In October 1857, Louis Philippe's daughter-in-law, Victoire, duchesse de Nemours, a Coburg cousin of the Queen and Prince Albert, gave birth to her second daughter Blanche at Claremont House. Queen Marie Amélie, Louis Philippe's consort, and her son, the duc de Nemours, visited the Queen and Prince 'and even expressed their joy that now the curse was taken from this house, that a healthy child had been born at Claremont, and that the mother was in excellent health'. But on 10 November the duchesse died, almost exactly forty years after Princess Charlotte. 'The relaxing treatment, so antagonistic to our English principles . . . may very likely have contributed to the catastrophe,' Prince Albert wrote to Stockmar (13 November 1857).

Leopold and Charlotte

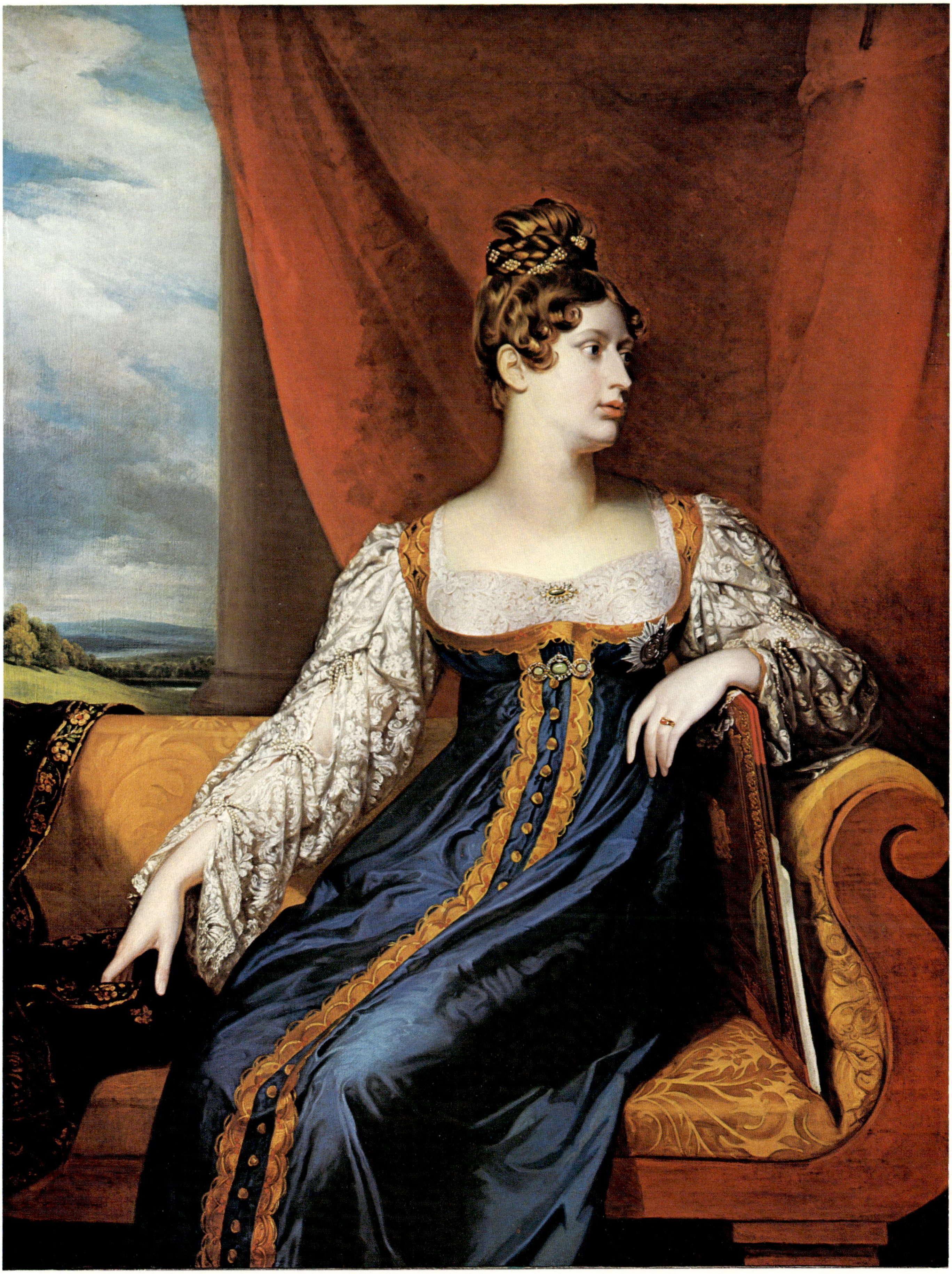

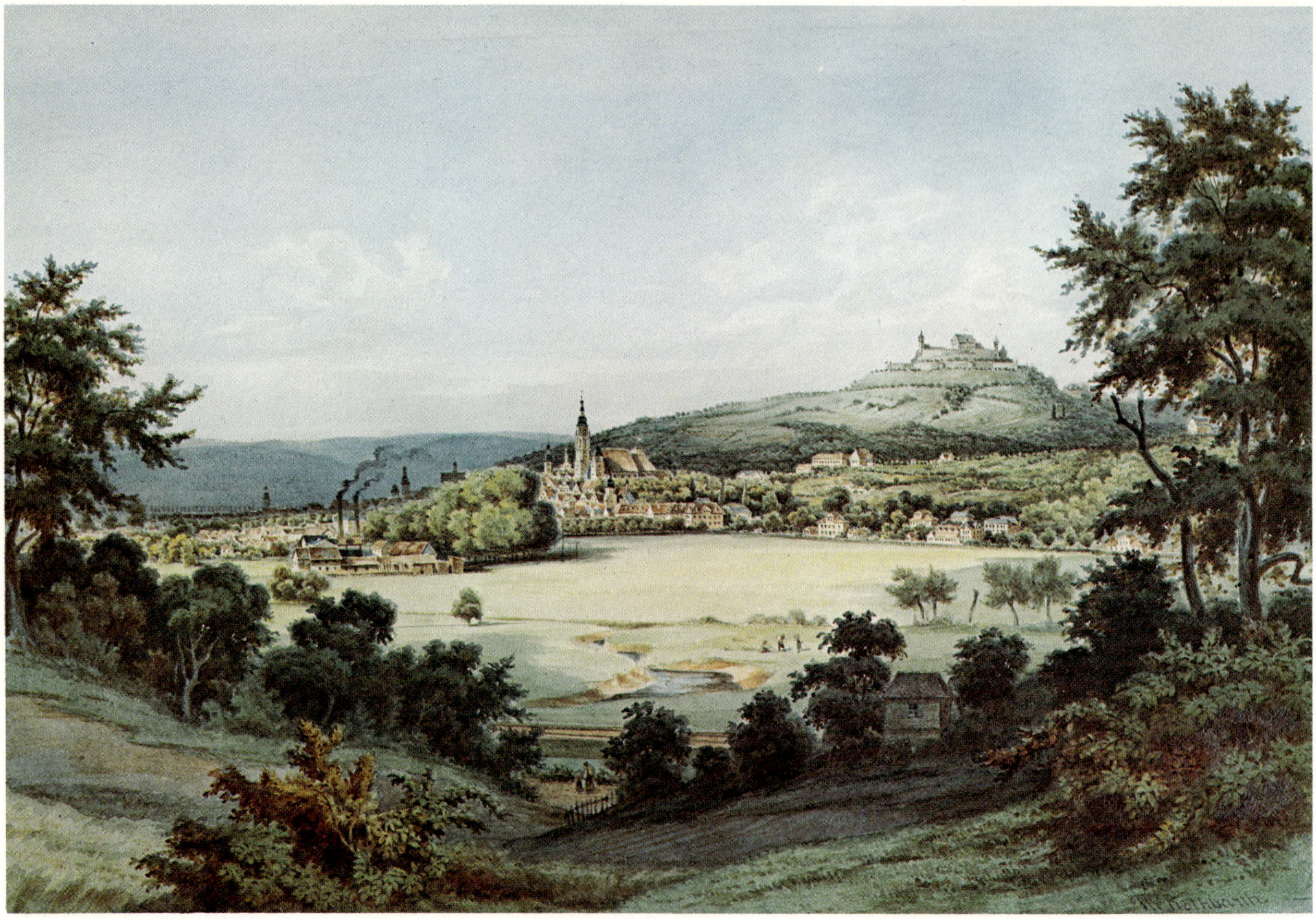

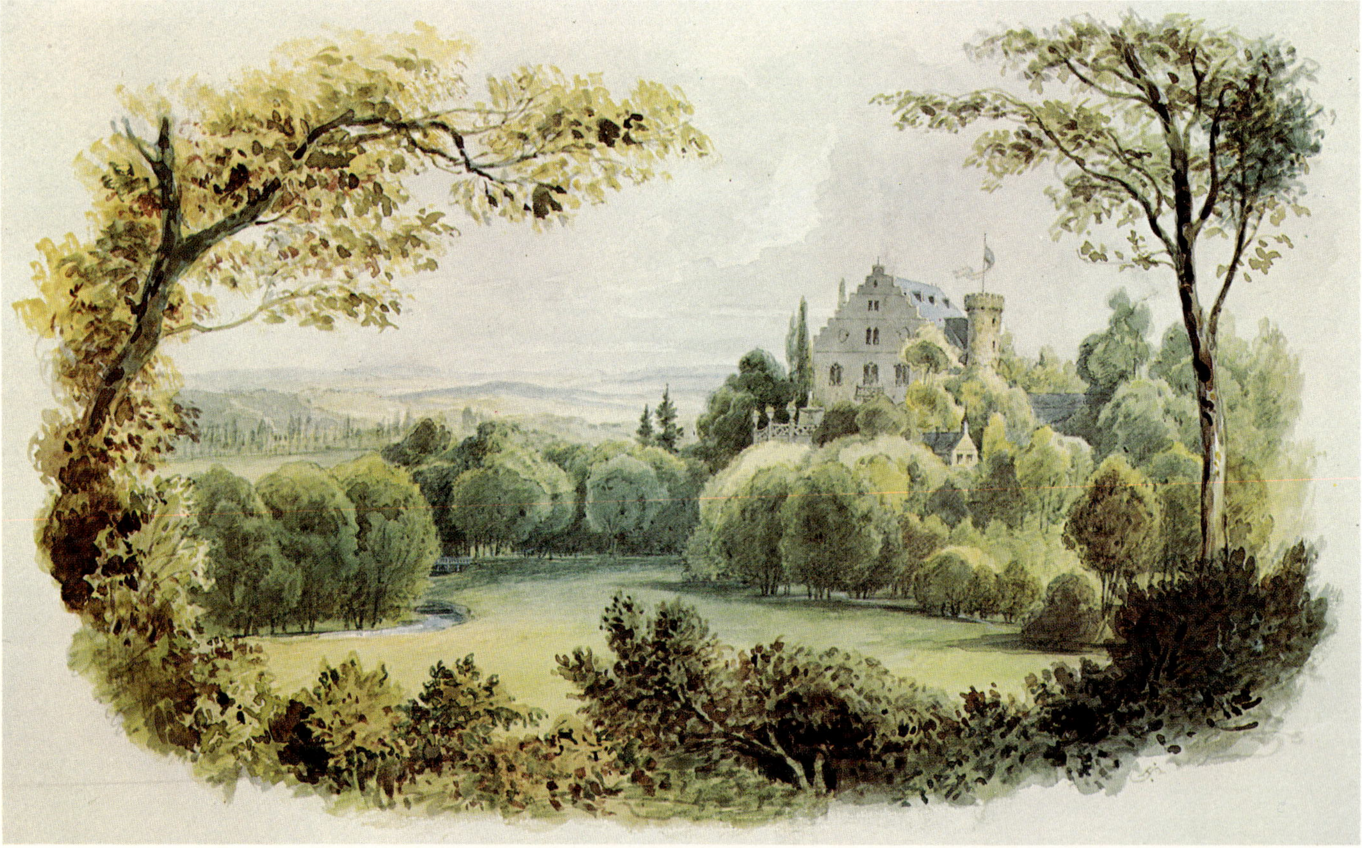

(*below*)
The Funeral Ceremony of the Princess Charlotte of Wales and of Saxe-Coburg taken from the Castle Hill, opposite the Market House, Windsor
Engraving by Thomas Sutherland after a painting by R. B. Davis (British Library)

Until the death in 1849 of Queen Adelaide, who left special instructions, it was customary for members of the Royal Family to be buried by night, which enhanced the atmosphere of gloom. Princess Charlotte's remains were brought from Claremont to be interred at St. George's Chapel, Windsor, and her body was laid beside that of her stillborn baby.

The Prince Regent was not present at his daughter's funeral, but Prince Leopold 'bore his bitter part in the ceremonial with manly dignity'. The procession in the chapel was conducted with great pomp, but there were unseemly squabbles regarding precedence and seating.

Medal
Issued to Commemorate the Death of Princess Charlotte, 6 November 1817 (British Museum)

The obverse depicts her bust and that of Prince Leopold; the reverse, inscribed 'Great Britain mourns: her Princes weep', depicts a funeral urn inscribed with the letter 'C' and a weeping willow. The medal expresses the general grief at the death of this beloved Princess and the quandary in which crown and nation were placed with regard to the succession.

(*opposite top*)
Coburg from the west
Watercolour by Ferdinand Rothbart (Royal Collection) *see chapter three*

This watercolour shows the small town of Coburg in its rural setting, dominated to the east by the Veste Coburg, on the right of the picture. The Veste Coburg, an early sixteenth-century fortress, was a residence of the Ernestine dukes until the Ehrenburg Palace was built in 1547, and in 1530 Luther stayed there and translated the Psalms. It was restored 1836–57. Leading up to the Veste Coburg from the town is the Hofgarten. Standing out in the town itself is the steeple of the Moritzkirche, while in the foreground on its edge is the 'Anger', the scene of popular festivals. The chimneys to the left are the gasworks, and the stream in the foreground is the Itz, while the blue hills of the Thüringer Wald stretch in the distance to Gotha.

(*opposite bottom*)
Rosenau from the Wolfsbach Valley
Watercolour by Heinrich Schneider (Royal Collection) *see chapter three*

'If I were not who I am—*this* would have been my real home, but I shall always consider it my second one', Queen Victoria wrote in her journal, 20 August 1845. In 1805 Francis, Duke of Coburg acquired the estate of Rosenau, four miles from Coburg, as part of a territorial exchange with August, Duke of Gotha. Francis's son, Duke Ernest I, inherited the shell of a house at Rosenau, and between 1809 and 1817 he built a little, yellow, pseudo-Gothic castle. With its large round tower and crow-step gables Rosenau recalled some of the older Scottish baronial castles, and, indeed, Prince Albert was to be reminded of Rosenau by the surrounding scenery at Balmoral.

Ernest I brought his young bride Louise of Gotha to the castle, where he staged a chivalrous tournament for her. She revelled in the Romantic setting. 'Beside the Schloss flows the Itz, chattering noisily over the stones. A little further on one comes to a huge waterfall tumbling over high rocks into a grotto. . . The scenery is so varied. . . The whole place is like a green garden,' she wrote home to Gotha.

Here the Duchess gave birth to her second son Albert, whose love for Rosenau matched that of his parents, and on their visit to Coburg in 1845, the Queen and Prince Albert were given the castle as a residence. On their next and final visit together in 1860 she wrote in her journal (26 September), 'It is all so lovely. Those fine meadows, valleys, hills and woods, and everywhere those very picturesque little farms and villages with red roofs and wooden beams.'

The artist, Heinrich Schneider (1811–1884), was appointed curator of the Ducal Picture Gallery and collection of engravings at Schloss Friedenstein, Gotha in 1849.

Leopold and Charlotte 19

H.M. The Queen
Engraving by C. E. Wagstaff after a painting by E. T. Parris, 1837 (British Museum)

In a letter to her sisters, dated 12 July 1837, Mrs. Sallie Coles Stevenson, wife of the American Minister in London, wrote, 'Now everyone is run mad with loyalty to the young Queen... In all societies nothing is talked about but her beauty, her wisdom, her gentleness & self-possession.' Prince Albert had already commented on his cousin Victoria's 'astonishing self-possession' in a letter to his father written on 4 July of the same year.

The Second Coburg Marriage: the Duke and Duchess of Kent

The death of Princess Charlotte placed the succession to the British crown in jeopardy. George III had seven sons and five daughters alive at this time, all in middle age, but Charlotte had been the only legitimate grandchild. Most of his sons were in financial difficulties and had established illicit liaisons, while his daughters were childless or unmarried. The new situation offered possibilities for the sons to rehabilitate their finances, since Parliament was expected to make generous settlements on royal marriages.

Within a year of Charlotte's death three of her uncles, the Dukes of Clarence, Kent and Cambridge, had made suitable marriages to German princesses and within a further year the three Duchesses, and also the Duchess of Cumberland, were all pregnant. The Duke of Kent had married Prince Leopold's sister Victoria, the widowed Princess of Leiningen. After the birth on 24 May 1819 of their daughter Alexandrina Victoria, named after her godfather Tsar Alexander I and her mother, the Kents wintered for reasons of economy at Sidmouth, where the Duke caught a chill and died (23 January 1820), to be followed within a week by his father, King George III.

The alien Duchess and her orphaned baby, who stood third in succession after her childless uncles, were penniless and quite alone, exposed to the hostility of the new King George IV, who only wished them out of the country. 'I know not what would have become of you and your Mama, if I had not then existed', her uncle Leopold wrote to Queen Victoria years later (7 January 1859). After the death of Princess Charlotte, Prince Leopold's first inclination had been to return to the Continent, but it was the perspicacious Stockmar who persuaded him to stay in England with his grief and so to obviate any peril to his £50,000 allowance. George IV was persuaded to permit the Duchess to return to Kensington Palace and there, with £3000 yearly allowance from Leopold the little Princess was able to grow up according to her father's wish as an Englishwoman. 'Uncle Leopold' became a substitute father for her.

A new and higher destiny, however, beckoned for Leopold, for after the Belgians revolted in 1830 against their Dutch king, they elected Leopold King of the Belgians in 1831. He then married Louise, the eldest daughter of the French King Louis Philippe. Well might the Prince of Orange execrate 'this man who has stolen my wife and my kingdom'. Leopold and Stockmar accordingly left London, and the Duchess of Kent came to rely increasingly on her ambitious comptroller, Sir John Conroy, who played on her fears of a plot by the Duke of Cumberland to displace her daughter from her position in the succession. The Duchess rejected invitations to court by King William IV, who had succeeded his brother, George IV, in 1830, and sought to become regent for her daughter even in the event of succession after her majority. Against this 'Kensington System' dominated by Conroy, the Princess Victoria could only rely on her Hanoverian governess Louise Lehzen, who thus established a very powerful position and worked closely with Lord Melbourne, the Prime Minister, after the Queen's accession on the death of her uncle, on 22 June 1837.

Victoria, Duchess of Kent (1786–1861) and Princess Victoria (1819–1901)
Painting by Sir William Beechey, 1822 (Royal Collection)

On the death of the Duke of Kent his widow determined to bring up their daughter according to his wishes. 'Stranger as I then was I became deeply impressed with the absolute necessity of bringing her up entirely in this country, that every feeling should be that of her native land, and proving thereby my devotion to duty by rejecting all those feelings of home and kindred that divided my heart,' she wrote in March 1830 when submitting an educational curriculum for approval to the Bishops of London and Lincoln.

Thanks to her brother Prince Leopold's allowance of £3000 per annum she was able to remain at Kensington Palace with her daughters Feodora of Leiningen and the Princess Victoria. The language of the household was English. Parliament granted her an additional allowance of £6000 in 1825. William IV and Queen Adelaide vainly sought to attract the Duchess and the Princess, then heiress presumptive, to court. The Regency Act of 1830 named the Duchess as regent in the event of her daughter's succession as a minor.

The Duchess, however, unfortunately relied excessively on Sir John Conroy who had been the Duke's equerry and who subsequently established a domination over the household. He played upon her fears of the Duke of Cumberland and so persuaded her to seek a regency despite the majority of her daughter (24 May 1837). This intimacy with Conroy and subservience to him, accentuated after Leopold went to Belgium, produced a rift between mother and daughter, with the Princess relying on her governess Lehzen, and led to an open alienation on Queen Victoria's accession. Conroy was generously pensioned off but was treated with complete personal disregard, while the young Queen showed more affection to Queen Adelaide than to her mother.

Edward, Duke of Kent (1767–1820)
Miniature by Paul Fischer after a painting by Sir William Beechey (Royal Collection)

Queen Victoria often referred proudly to herself as 'a Soldier's Daughter'. George III's fourth son spent his early life in the Army becoming Commander-in-Chief of British North America and Governor of Gibraltar. As a young man in Geneva he made the acquaintance of Julie de Montgenêt, baronne de Fortisson, a French refugee whose husband was killed in 1794. A most respectable woman, she subsequently became his companion under the name of Madame de Saint-Laurent for some twenty years in Canada, Gibraltar and England. From his earliest military life he incurred debts which accumulated and pursued him throughout life, and in order to improve his financial position he determined to marry in the hope that Parliament would make him a generous allowance. Princess Charlotte and her husband suggested that he should wed Prince Leopold's sister Victoria, the widowed Princess of Leiningen, resident at Amorbach. They were married in Coburg on 29 May 1818 and again according to Anglican rites at the Chapel Royal in July in a double ceremony with the Duke of Clarence, who succeeded to the throne as William IV. Parliament proved less generous than he had hoped and so they returned to Amorbach.

During his service at Gibraltar the Duke had been told by a Spanish gipsy that he would have a daughter who would be a great Queen. When the Duchess became pregnant he determined to obviate any queries regarding legitimacy by ensuring that the birth took place in England. For reasons of economy he himself drove one of the coaches which carried his wife, her daughter Feodora of Leiningen and the celebrated German gynaecologist Charlotte von Siebold to England. On 24 May 1819 at Kensington Palace the Duchess gave birth to a daughter, Alexandrina Victoria, 'white and round like a stuffed dove'. The Duke's financial worries continued and so the family went to Sidmouth for the winter. There the Duke caught a chill and was dead within a fortnight (23 January 1820).

22 The Duke and Duchess of Kent

Charles, Prince of Leiningen (1804–1856)
Miniature by Sir William Ross (Royal Collection)

Charles's father, Charles Emich, Prince of Leiningen, had been compensated in 1803 with the abbey of Amorbach for lands annexed to the French Republic. In 1806 he lost his 'immediate' sovereignty, and his lands were mediatized under Bavaria and Baden. Despite the loss of sovereign status the mediatized princes continued to rank as *ebenbürtig*, i.e. qualified to marry into sovereign houses.

Prince Charles succeeded his father in 1814 under the regency of his mother Victoria of Saxe-Coburg. When she married the Duke of Kent and went to England in 1819 he remained in Germany and was therefore less in touch than his sister Feodora with their half-sister, the future Queen Victoria. Charles of Leiningen visited England in 1825 with Duchess Augusta of Coburg, but in 1836, by lending his support to Conroy in his attempt to persuade Victoria to accept a regency, he somewhat alienated his half-sister.

The mediatization of south and west German princes contrasted with the success of the minor north German princes in retaining their sovereignty. As a consequence the mediatized houses were generally more ready to accept fusion in a German national state. Prince Charles became a strong supporter of the more radical movement for national unity and took a leading part in the activities of the Frankfurt National Assembly. He was nominated as first German prime minister in August 1848 by the regent, Archduke John of Austria. He resigned in September, however, when the Great Powers obliged the German forces to give way to the Danes in Schleswig-Holstein. His marriage to Countess Marie von Klebelsberg, a lady of lower social standing, proved unhappy and ended in divorce.

Prince Charles's selfish hedonism was very repugnant to Prince Albert who saw in it an example to be avoided by his own son. Nevertheless Prince Albert wrote to his brother Ernest, 'Karl was, you might say, the representative of our youth and of the Coburg family: the link between Papa, Uncle Leopold and Mamma, between Germany and the West—and certainly it was not possible for anyone to be more amiable and agreeable as a companion than he was. Our children mourn for him with all their heart, as Uncle Charles was their great favourite' (14 November 1856).

Feodora of Leiningen, Princess of Hohenlohe-Langenburg (1807–1872)
Miniature by Sir William Ross, 1835 (Royal Collection)

Princess Feodora, the Duchess of Kent's daughter by her first marriage, was twelve years older than her half-sister Queen Victoria, but there was always a close bond of affection between them, sometimes seeming to arouse Prince Albert's jealousy. She was devoted to her step-father the Duke of Kent and came to live at Kensington with him and her mother. Louise Lehzen was originally her governess, and, as with Princess Victoria, English was always spoken. Like her sister later, she found life at Kensington Palace very constrictive and was glad in 1828 to marry Ernest, Prince of Hohenlohe-Langenburg, a cousin of Queen Adelaide. The marriage proved very happy and there were five children.

Princess Feodora was a most kind, affectionate and devout woman. Though she spent her married life in south Germany she always felt herself an Englishwoman and wrote to Queen Victoria of 'our beloved country. It is my heart's and mind's country, in which all my interests are centred' (27 February 1853). She always enjoyed English company. She transmitted this love of England to her children, and her youngest son, Victor, entered the Royal Navy and on marrying Admiral Seymour's daughter assumed the title Count Gleichen after a family estate in Coburg. His children changed their name to Gibbs during the First World War.

The Princess Royal wrote to her mother from Berlin, 'Aunt Feodora is my comfort, to her I can talk more unreservedly than to anyone' (1 March 1858). On the birth of the future Kaiser William II, Princess Feodora congratulated the Queen writing, 'Oh, if only on all subjects the two nations would feel and act together' (5 February 1859). The Kaiser was later to marry Augusta Victoria of Schleswig-Holstein, the daughter of Feodora's own daughter Adelaide, whom Napoleon III had originally sought in marriage.

The Duke and Duchess of Kent 23

Charlotte Heidenreich-von Siebold, née Heiland (1788–1859)
Painting by Franz Hubert Müller, 1819 (Bückeburg, Collection of Frau Lotte Velte)

Charlotte von Siebold assisted at the births of both Queen Victoria and Prince Albert. Her mother, Josepha Henning, studied and practised midwifery after her second marriage to Dr. Damian von Siebold, a member of a distinguished medical family. In 1815 the University of Giessen granted her an honorary doctorate 'in arte obstetricia', making her the second German woman to obtain such a distinction.

Charlotte began her own medical studies under the supervision of her mother and step-father, whom she assisted, and attended lectures at the University of Göttingen. In 1814 she qualified in midwifery at Darmstadt. In March 1817 she broke fresh ground by being the first German woman to obtain a doctorate in medicine after publicly defending her thesis, on obstetrics, before a large and distinguished audience at the University of Giessen. Her Göttingen teacher, the celebrated Professor F. B. Osiander, was the principal German protagonist of the operational method and opposed the more conservative English techniques. While Charlotte recognized in her thesis the value of the forceps, she emphasized the desirability of their restricted use, eliciting Osiander's comment on his copy of her thesis that pregnancy became women better than writing about that condition.

Charlotte von Siebold soon acquired a wide reputation, and in 1818 she was called to Coburg to assist at the birth of the future Duke Ernest II. She was there during the wedding of the Duke of Kent. Her leaning towards English methods and the ever-present memory of Princess Charlotte's death possibly prompted the Duke to employ her to travel with him and his wife from Amorbach to Kensington to attend at the birth there of Princess Victoria in May 1819. He was taking no chances comparable to those of the Duchess of Clarence, who had been attended at her confinement in March by a distinguished army surgeon and lost her baby the same day, the Duke of Clarence having a strong distrust of German physicians. Dr. Siebold then went to Coburg to attend Duchess Louise in her second confinement, for Prince Albert.

When Queen Victoria and Prince Albert visited Mainz in 1845 Charlotte von Siebold, who had married Dr. Heidenreich in 1829, was presented to them. In the same year she wrote to the Grand Duke of Hesse-Darmstadt describing the deplorable circumstances of many of her patients. After her death in 1859 a group of ladies in Darmstadt founded the 'Heidenreich-von Siebold Stiftung' to provide assistance in such cases, and the Queen and Prince Albert subscribed to its endowment. After her marriage to Prince Louis of Hesse-Darmstadt, their daughter Princess Alice became its patroness. She took a thorough interest in the work of the foundation, visiting some of the cases. Despite her debt to Charlotte von Siebold, the Queen never approved of young women pursuing medical studies alongside men.

Louise, Baroness Lehzen (1784–1870)
Miniature by C. F. Koepke (Royal Collection)

Louise Lehzen, Queen Victoria's governess, became the chief confidante and greatest formative influence on the Queen in her early years; 'Lehzen is my greatest friend.' The daughter of a Hanoverian pastor, with strong loyalties to the royal House of Guelph, she was employed by the Duke of Kent, shortly before his death, as governess to the Duchess's daughter Feodora with the idea that she should later educate his own baby daughter. She brought up both her charges to be Englishwomen. 'There was great devotedness in her but not much softness and yet how attached we were to her, and had all right to be so', Princess Feodora wrote to the Queen after Lehzen's death. 'I owed her much and she adored me', Queen Victoria wrote to the Princess Royal (8 October 1870). Lehzen was created a Hanoverian baroness in 1826 by King George IV.

After the Queen's accession she exercised considerable jurisdiction in the royal palaces and was a strong supporter of Lord Melbourne. This brought her into conflict with Prince Albert; 'Lehzen is a crazy, common, stupid intriguer.' With the help of Baron Stockmar he prevailed on the Queen to pension her off in 1842, and, henceforward, there was no domestic rival to the Prince. She retired to Bückeburg, near Hanover, and saw the Queen in Gotha in 1845 and again at Reinhardsbrunn in 1862.

(*opposite*)
King William IV (1765–1837)
Painting by Sir Thomas Lawrence (Royal Collection)

William IV, the 'Sailor King', entered the Navy in 1779 and served at New York, the last British foothold in the Thirteen Colonies, at Gibraltar and in the West Indies, where he met Nelson and gave the bride away at his wedding. Nelson wrote of him, 'In every respect both as a man and a Prince, I love him' (9 February 1787). The Prince was created Duke of Clarence in 1789 and retired from active naval service in 1790 as a rear-admiral. In the same year he took up residence at Bushey with the actress Dorothea Jordan, by whom he had ten children, the Fitzclarences. This liaison was terminated in 1811, and the Duke cast about for a suitable marriage. In 1818 in a double ceremony with the Duke and Duchess of Kent, he married Adelaide of Saxe-Meiningen, who exercised a most beneficent influence on him.

Although he harboured a certain jealousy of the girl who would one day succeed him, the King had considerable affection for Princess Victoria and desired that she should play her rôle at court, resenting the Duchess of Kent's determination to keep her away. He was addicted to making tactless and often irrelevant speeches but never more so than on his last birthday (21 August 1836) when he announced in the presence of both the Princess and the Duchess that 'I trust in God that my life may be spared for nine months longer, after which period, in the event of my death, no regency would take place' by 'a person now near me, who is herself incompetent to act with propriety in the station in which she would be placed.' Politically he favoured Peel and the Tories rather more than Melbourne and the Whigs.

He disliked Prince, later King, Leopold and sought to veto the visit of Leopold's nephews Ernest and Albert of Saxe-Coburg in 1836 as he feared a scheme to marry one of them to Victoria. He favoured instead her marriage to her cousin Prince George of Cambridge, who had spent some of his formative years with William IV and Queen Adelaide, or to Alexander, second son of the Prince of Orange. Queen Victoria was fond of the King and wrote in her journal, 'He was odd, very odd and singular, but his intentions were often ill-interpreted.'

24 *The Duke and Duchess of Kent*

William IV: Peace and Affection to All
Silhouette drawn and engraved by L. Bruce (British Museum)

Queen Adelaide (1792–1849)
Miniature by Sir William Ross (Royal Collection)

Adelaide of Saxe-Meiningen married William, Duke of Clarence, twenty-seven years older than herself, in 1818. He had spent his life in the Navy, which had shaped his manners, and had fathered ten Fitzclarences by the actress Dorothea Jordan. His wife had a remarkable reformative effect on him and was prepared to be a mother to his illegitimate children, who all too frequently repaid her in unpardonable fashion. Her own two daughters died in infancy and so her strong maternal instincts were perforce extended to Prince George of Cambridge and to the younger members of her own and her husband's family.

When the Duke of Kent died she went daily to console the widowed Duchess and wrote to her, 'My children are dead, but your child lives and she is mine too.' Nevertheless her relations with the Duchess of Kent became severely strained. Queen Adelaide was always most kind and generous to Princess Victoria, who reciprocated with the utmost affection and consideration after her accession. She wrote on the dowager Queen's death to King Leopold (11 December 1849), 'We have lost the kindest and dearest of friends, and the *universal* feeling of sorrow, of regret and of *real* appreciation of her character is very touching and gratifying... Much was done to set Mamma against her, but the dear Queen ever forgave this, ever showed love and affection, and for the last eight years their friendship was as great as ever.'

Talleyrand's niece, the duchesse de Dino, paid tribute to her perfect simplicity, truth and uprightness. 'I have rarely seen a person more devoted to duty. She is both kind and cheerful, and though not beautiful she is perfectly graceful.' Adelaide remained, however, very German in character and was inclined to talk German excessively in the presence of English people, which sometimes gave offence. When Prince Albert and his brother visited London in 1836 they were coolly received by King William IV, but the Queen showed them great kindness, and after his marriage he shared Victoria's affection and esteem for her aunt.

The Duke and Duchess of Kent 25

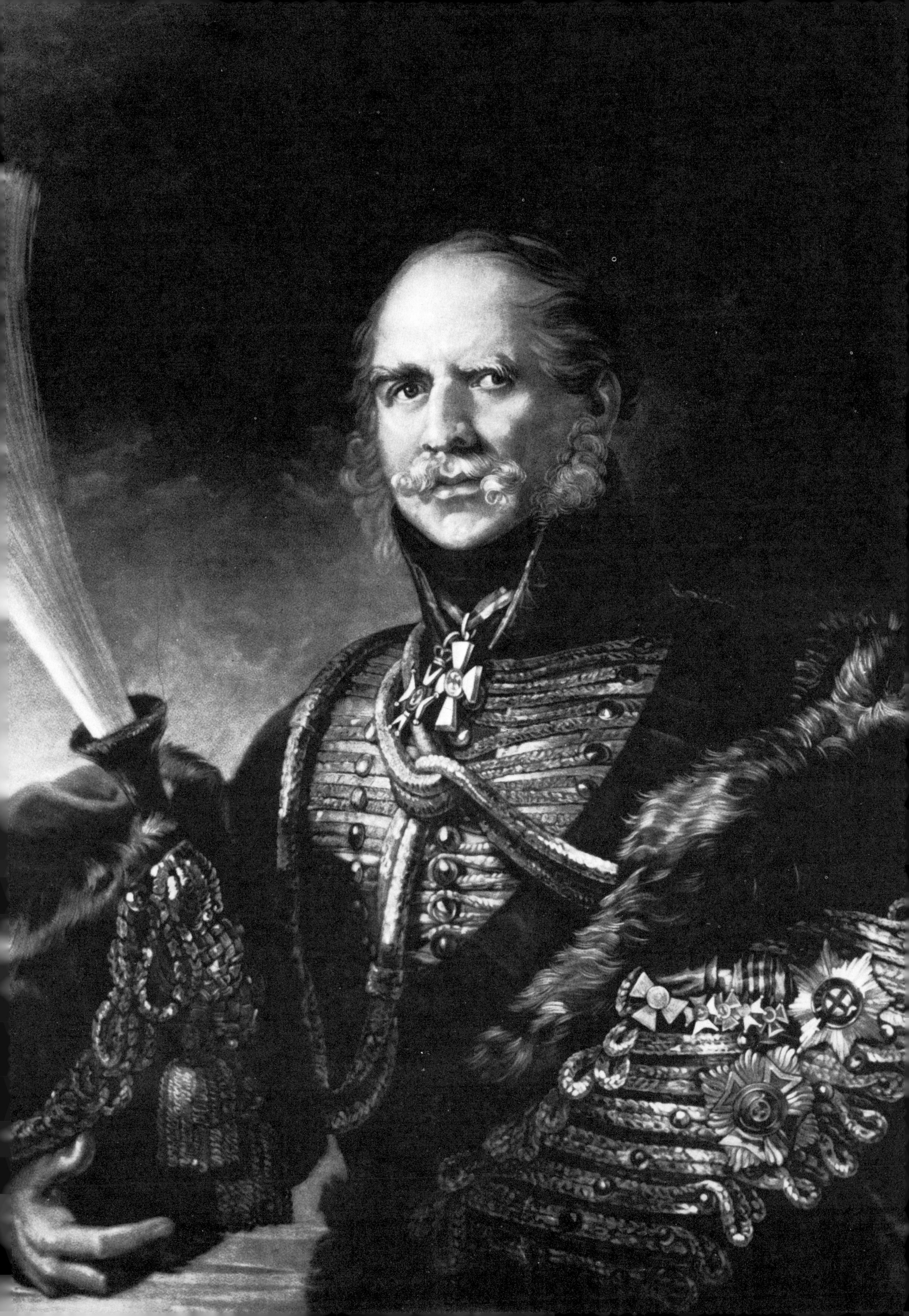

Ernest Augustus, King of Hanover, Duke of Cumberland (1771–1851)
Engraving by Henry Dawe after a painting by George Dawe (British Museum)

The fifth son of George III, Prince Ernest Augustus was a pillar of ultra-reactionary Toryism, his political views having been determined by his experience of the French Revolution. This, combined with questionable aspects of his private life, made him extremely unpopular in England. Cumberland was next in succession to Princess Victoria, and the Duchess of Kent constantly feared that he might seek to displace her. On her accession in 1837 to the English throne he succeeded to the crown of Hanover which passed only in the male line. The new King immediately suspended the liberal constitution of 1833, with its assimilation of the royal and the state budget, granted by King William IV, to which as heir presumptive Ernest Augustus had objected at the time. This provoked the protest and dismissal of the seven professors of Göttingen University and aroused a storm of indignation among the supporters of German unity and constitutionalism, including Prince Albert, then at Bonn University. It is ironic to note that Prince Albert and King Leopold were later to protest, as agnates, on grounds very analogous to those of King Ernest Augustus, against a similar budgetary assimilation in the Coburg constitution of 1849.

As King of Hanover and a Prince of the Blood Royal, Ernest Augustus claimed precedence over Prince Albert in England, and this led to disagreeable incidents, especially at the wedding of Princess Augusta of Cambridge in 1843, so that the Queen termed him 'an old wretch'. He also refused to supply the Queen with the cream and black Hanoverian horses which since the time of George I habitually drew the English royal coach on state occasions and furthermore laid claim to certain of the royal jewels as pertaining to Hanover. After examination by three Law Lords a final decision substantially in favour of Hanover was given in 1857, much to the chagrin of the Queen and Prince. The King was also affronted by his niece's refusal to permit the conferment of the Hanoverian Guelphic Order on her subjects.

King Ernest Augustus succeeded by concessions in riding the revolutionary storms of 1848 but opposed the national unity movement supported by the Coburgs. In 1866 it was the forces of Duke Ernest II before Gotha, which barred the southward retreat of King George V of Hanover, Ernest Augustus's son, and his army, wasting precious hours in negotiations and so forcing their surrender. This led to the annexation of Hanover by Prussia.

After painting the portrait of the Duke of Kent in 1818, George Dawe (1781–1829) followed him to the Continent where he painted Ernest I, Duke of Coburg. He worked at Berlin, where the Duke of Cumberland was then residing, and, after painting the portrait of the Grand Duchess Alexandra Feodorovna, the Prussian wife of the later Tsar Nicholas I, was invited to St. Petersburg in 1819. He remained there until shortly before his death and was joined by Henry Dawe (1790–1848), whose engravings served to make his elder brother's portraits more widely known.

Prince George of Cambridge, later Duke of Cambridge (1819–1904)
Engraving by William Ward after a painting by John Lucas, dedicated to Queen Adelaide, 1837 (British Museum)

The only son of Adolphus, Duke of Cambridge, Prince George was the first grandchild of George III to be born after the death of Princess Charlotte. His father was Governor General of Hanover from 1814 until the succession to the Hanoverian throne of the Duke of Cumberland in 1837. He was sent to England in 1830 and grew up at the court of William IV and Queen Adelaide, who lavished affection on him which he fully reciprocated. Their hope that he would marry Princess Victoria was widely shared in England but there was no mutual attraction. Once the Queen's marriage had been arranged he married morganatically in January 1840 the actress Louisa Fairbrother, known as Mrs. Fitzgeorge, by whom he had three sons.

He was devoted to the Army and had a distinguished military career, commanding the division which won the victory of the Alma in September 1854. Invalided home from the Crimea, the Prince became in 1856 the last Commander-in-Chief of the Army, and, after the death of Prince Albert, he was called upon to undertake many royal duties. He became Duke of Cambridge in 1850 on the death of his father. His sister Mary Adelaide married the Duke of Teck and became the mother of Queen Mary.

The Duke and Duchess of Kent

The Tsarevitch, later Alexander II, Tsar of Russia (1818–1881)
Lithograph by J. C. Schall after a painting by Franz Krüger (British Museum)

In June 1839 the young Tsarevitch Alexander, son and heir to Nicholas I, Tsar of Russia, visited England. He was reputed one of the handsomest princes in Europe, modest and gracious. The marquis de Custine in his penetrating analysis of Russia in that year said that the future Tsar would 'obtain obedience through the constraint of a gracious character rather than by terror'.

He charmed the young Queen Victoria when she gave a ball in his honour at Windsor. She danced the mazurka with him, and her sensual emotions were tingled. She wrote in her journal, 'I never enjoyed myself more. I got to bed by a $\frac{1}{4}$ to 3 but could not sleep till 5. I really am quite in love with the Grand Duke.' The Cesarevich race at Newmarket commemorates his visit in 1839. The Queen did not meet him again until 1874 after his only daughter had married the Queen's second son, Alfred, Duke of Edinburgh. She found him terribly altered, sad and careworn. 'It is just thirty five years that I took leave of him here, at Windsor, in June!'

Franz Krüger (1797–1857) was the leading military and portrait painter of Berlin. He visited St. Petersburg four times to fulfil commissions for Nicholas I.

(*opposite*)
William Lamb, second Viscount Melbourne (1779–1848)
Painting by John Partridge, 1844 (National Portrait Gallery)

William Lamb was an aristocrat in every sense of the word. Bred into a society untrammelled by conventions, he developed into a highly cultivated but very paradoxical character, blending extreme sensitivity on the one hand with an almost cynical unawareness on the other. A sceptic in an increasingly industrialized society, he questioned the ultimate benefits of reform.

Melbourne entered Parliament in 1806. Originally a Whig, he supported Canning who made him Secretary for Ireland, a post he held from 1827 to 1828. With the other Canningites, he joined the Whigs under Lord Grey and was Home Secretary from 1830 to 1834, fulfilling this office, as Charles Greville remarked, very inefficiently compared with Peel. He was appointed Prime Minister for the first time in 1834 and again in 1835. Shortly before William IV died, Sir Robert Peel remarked to Greville that the future Queen would do well to rely entirely upon the advice of Melbourne. Fortunately for Melbourne, and ultimately for Queen Victoria herself, this was exactly what she did. Theirs was an idyllic relationship. She was completely captivated by his charm and quick to appreciate his invaluable knowledge of both political and social affairs. When Melbourne resigned in 1839 Peel found himself at a considerable disadvantage, and the Queen did everything in her power during the crisis over the proposed appointment of certain Tory instead of Whig Ladies of the Bedchamber in order to ensure the reinstatement of Melbourne as her Prime Minister until 1841. With the advent of Prince Albert, Melbourne's influence diminished. He died in retirement at Brocket Hall in 1848.

28 The Duke and Duchess of Kent

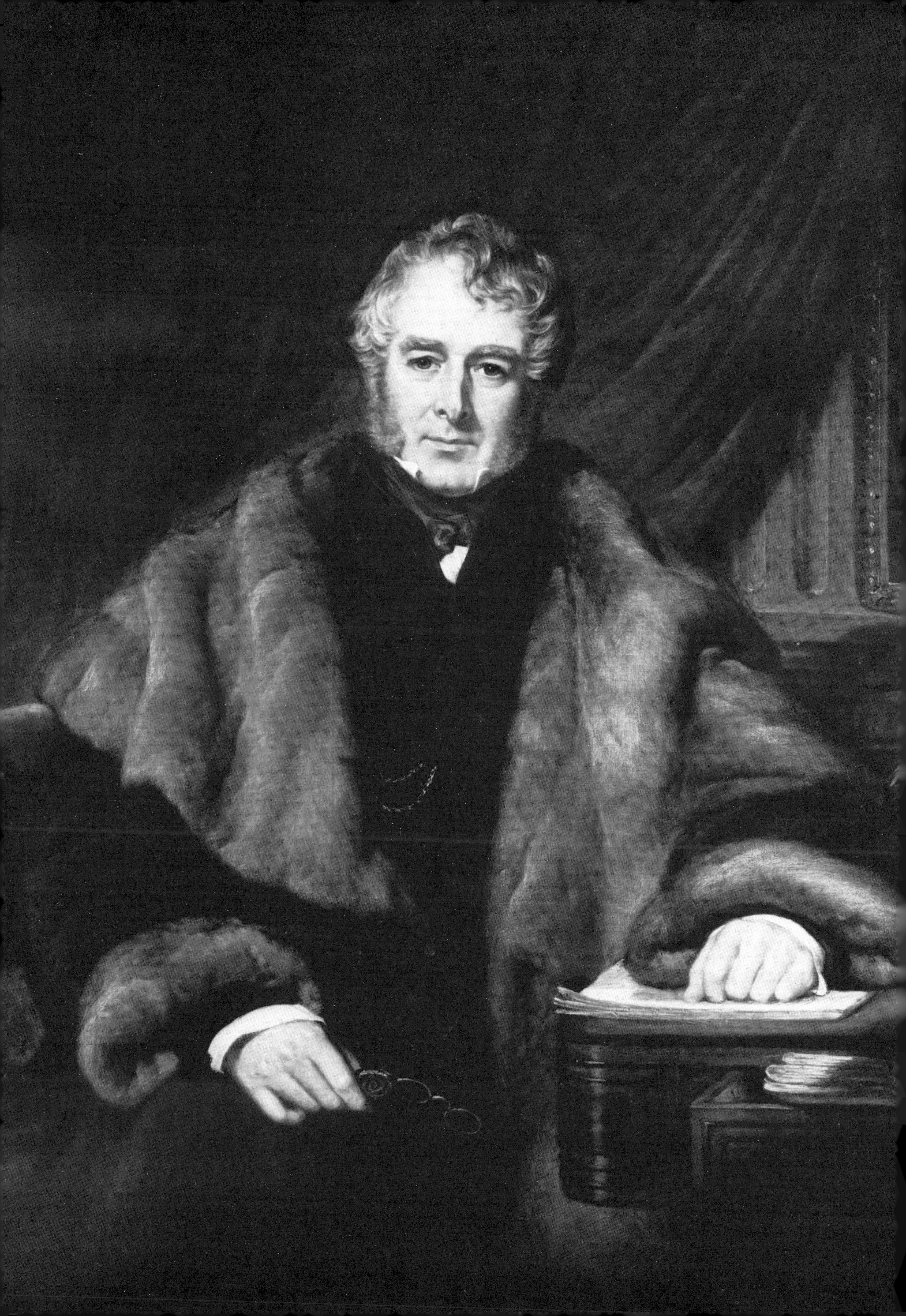

Prince Albert in 1839
Engraving after a miniature by Sir William Ross (British Museum)

'He certainly is a very beautiful young man, a thorough German, and a fine poetical specimen of the race.' Thus commented Caroline Fox, a Quaker relation of Elizabeth Fry, the prison reformer, who was present at the meeting in Exeter Hall, London, on 1 June 1840, at which the Prince, as President of the Society for the Extinction of the Slave Trade, made his maiden speech as the Queen's husband. The address was prepared with the assistance of his secretary George Anson and Stockmar and was then learnt by heart by Prince Albert. In his patronage of this society Prince Albert was following in the footsteps of the Queen's father, the late Duke of Kent.

The Prince's style of dress in this engraving, with open collar, was popularized by the poet Schiller and was known familiarly as the 'Schillerkragen'.

Albert of Saxe-Coburg: the Grooming Years

Prince Albert of Saxe-Coburg was born at the castle of Rosenau near Coburg on 26 August 1819. He and his elder brother Ernest were named after the two brothers in the fifteenth century who were the progenitors of the Ernestine and Albertine lines of the House of Wettin. They were the only children of Ernest I, Duke of Saxe-Coburg-Saalfeld and his wife Louise, only child of the Duke of Saxe-Gotha. The marriage, at first happy, turned sour owing to the infidelities of the Duke, and the Duchess left Coburg and their two sons when the boys were five and four years old. They never saw her again although they treasured her memory. The young Princes were brought up by their tutor Christoph Florschütz, and Albert especially responded with enthusiasm to a tough academic curriculum. Although the brothers were neither bodily nor mentally much alike, the bond between them was particularly intimate. 'From our earliest years we shared every joy and sorrow together as they came,' wrote Duke Ernest II, and this confiding of thoughts and plans continued after separation.

Their life as boys centred around Coburg and Gotha, whose duchy their father inherited in 1826 on the extinction of its ducal line. They divided their time between Rosenau and the Ehrenburg Palace at Coburg, Schloss Friedenstein at Gotha and Reinhardsbrunn with visits to their two doting grandmothers, Duchess Augusta of Coburg at Ketschendorf and Duchess Caroline of Gotha at Friedrichsthal.

In April 1835 the two Princes were confirmed, marking the religious end of childhood and the entry into adult life. In the following year their education at Coburg gave way to university study and foreign travel, and after brief visits to Kensington Palace and to King Louis Philippe in Paris, they went to Brussels in June 1836 to visit their uncle, King Leopold.

As a training ground for constitutional monarchy Belgium was particularly apt. With its two language groups, Flemings and Walloons, it had obtained its freedom from the Netherlands thanks to an alliance of antagonistic Catholics and Liberals, although war still continued until 1839. It enjoyed the protection of Britain and France but the stern disapproval of Russia and the eastern powers, who supported the legitimist claims of the King of the Netherlands. Belgium's constitution was extremely liberal, albeit with strong property qualifications for voting, and its industries rivalled those of Britain and France. Within the framework created by these heterogeneous and conflicting elements the King, advised by Baron von Stockmar, had to play out his key rôle.

The two young Princes met leading figures in the political, cultural and artistic life of the Belgian capital and also learned to appreciate early Flemish painting. Their most prominent tutor was Lambert Quételet, whose mathematical and statistical teaching on the law of probabilities was to have an enduring effect on Prince Albert's attitude to events. 'During his entire lifetime he preserved the statistically mechanical grasp of social and political questions' imbibed from Quételet, wrote his brother. They also received some military training and even mixed with Italian Carbonarist exiles.

In May 1837 the brothers went to study at Bonn University and joined the aristocratic 'Borussia' Corps. Prince Albert specialized in law and history and was much drawn to August Wilhelm von Schlegel, the translator of Shakespeare, and to the patriotic poet Ernst Moritz Arndt, noted for his violent Francophobia. Bonn University was a hotbed of German patriotic enthusiasm, and the Coburg Princes imbibed it in full measure. Albert was influenced by Professor Bethmann-Hollweg, a follower of Savigny's Historicism and by Immanuel Fichte, Professor of Philosophy, who regarded the principles of real conservatism as those of constant well-planned reform, while all revolution consisted either in attempts to precipitate the future prematurely or to return to effete ideas, the last being only the chrysalis state of the first. These views were to bear fruit in Prince Albert's attitude to English politics and perhaps in the understanding he established with Peel.

During Prince Albert's period in Bonn two issues dominated the German political scene, the suspension of the Hanoverian constitution by the new king, Ernest Augustus, with its martyrization of the seven Göttingen professors who protested, and the arrest of the Archbishop of Cologne by the Prussian government for his stand on mixed marriages. The Coburg Princes were enthusiastically opposed to the King of Hanover while supporting the King of Prussia. In addition the German-Danish conflict over Schleswig-Holstein, which was later to affect so intimately the family life of Albert and Victoria, was already looming on the horizon. By September 1838, therefore, the political concepts of the Queen's future consort had been largely moulded on the Rhine.

On their return to Coburg Ernest went to Dresden for military training, while Albert set out for cultural study in Italy in the company of Baron von Stockmar, who thus first impinged on his life, and of Lieutenant Seymour of the British Army. This young officer, later General Sir Francis Seymour, was seconded for this duty at the special request of the King of the Belgians. By this means Prince Albert was able to improve his fluency in the English language and to acquaint himself better with English ways, both given high priority among his necessary accomplishments. After the Prince's marriage, Seymour was appointed Groom-in-Waiting to him.

From Prince Albert's babyhood Duchess Augusta of Coburg had envisaged the 'English Mayflower' as the bride for her grandson, but it was her son, King Leopold, with his adlatus Stockmar, who was to achieve the realization of the plan. In March 1838 on a visit to Brussels a conversation took place between King Leopold and Albert which was decisive for the latter's future. 'For the first time the English marriage was seriously spoken of,' wrote Duke Ernest II. There is something reminiscent of Goethe's *Wilhelm Meister* in the way in which the marriage was schemed with preparations so skilfully concealed as to leave full scope for the romance of voluntary choice. King Leopold wrote to the Queen (13 April 1838), 'It is my *great anxiety* to see Albert a *very good* and *distinguished young man* and *no pains will be thought too much* on my part if this end can be attained.' He wrote to Stockmar in March 1838 of the plan to marry Albert to Victoria, 'If he does not from the very outset accept it as a vocation of grave responsibility on the efficient fulfilment of which his honour and happiness depend, there is small likelihood of his succeeding.'

Stockmar, with his thoroughgoing mind, took over the celibate youth whom Florschütz had prepared and with systematic sagacity he set out to raise him to a very high ideal. He wrote to the Prince (7 May 1841), 'What I have seen during the time I have recently passed with you, strengthens me in the hope of achieving more or less the ideal for your future, which I set up for myself twenty months since.' The Queen of England's prospective husband was being envisaged and prepared like Tamino in Mozart's *The Magic Flute*.

Sir John Conroy told Princess Lieven that from 1835 on King Leopold had plotted with Lehzen to deprive the Duchess of Kent of all influence over her daughter in order that his alone should prevail. But the governess had profited rather than the King and now she would not 'allow' the Queen to marry (letter from Princess Lieven to Lady Cowper, 27 July 1839).

Albert had written from Bonn to congratulate his cousin on her accession, but after that their correspondence flagged. Yet King Leopold always kept his objective in view and wrote to Stockmar in March 1838 of 'the position Albert will occupy in England'. Accession to the throne had given the Queen unaccustomed liberty and with it came her close contact with the courtly Melbourne who filled the rôle of the father she had never known. Despite the urgings from her uncles Leopold and Ernest she was in no hurry to be married for three or four years and dreaded the thought of marriage and having to accommodate herself to another person. Yet the visit of her uncle Ferdinand of Coburg-Kohary with his three children in June 1839 made her realize her need for young company.

On 12 July the Queen told Lord Melbourne she had no great wish to see Albert, 'There was no engagement between us, I said, but that the young man was aware that there was the possibility of such a union. I said it wasn't right to keep him on, and not right to decide before they came.' The visit was disagreeable to her and she wished if possible never to marry. Three days later Victoria wrote pointedly to King Leopold, 'First of all, I wish to know if *Albert* is aware of the wish of his *Father* and *you* relative to *me*? Secondly if he knows that there is *no engagement* between us? I am anxious that you should acquaint Uncle Ernest, that if I should like Albert, that I can make *no final promise this year*, for at the *very earliest*, any such event could not take place till *two or three years hence*.' She added, 'Though all the reports of Albert are most favourable, and though I have little doubt I shall like him, still one can never answer beforehand for *feelings*, and I may not have the *feeling* for him which is requisite to ensure happiness.' She concluded, 'I am *very* anxious that it should be understood that I am *not* guilty of any breach of promise, for *I never gave any*.' For these reasons the Queen sought to postpone the proposed visit of her two Coburg cousins.

Albert knew that Victoria was said to be 'increasingly stubborn', delighting in etiquette, court ceremonies and late nights, all of which were anathema to him. So hesitation increased on his part too. There were delays in the visit and these led the Queen to write to King Leopold, 'I think they don't exhibit much empressement to come here, which rather shocks me.' For meanwhile flattering reports on Albert had come to her from their mutual cousin Alexander von Mensdorff, whom she considered 'a very correct observer of persons' whose opinion could be relied on.

So on 10 October 1839, after a rough crossing, which renewed his 'disgust for the sea', Albert came again to England determined that his cousin must make up her mind. Meanwhile the Queen herself was developing an increasing independence and reluctance to do so. However on Albert's arrival Victoria found him *'beautiful'* and *'very fascinating'*, and by the fifteenth she had announced to him, 'That it would make me *too happy* if he would consent to what I wished. I told him that it *was* a great sacrifice on his part but he would not allow it.' In the afternoon she wrote to Stockmar, 'All was settled between us this morning. I feel certain he will make me very happy. I wish I felt as certain of *my* making him happy, but I shall do my best.' Albert too wrote to Stockmar and received a homily on the worthy discharge of his prospective exalted duties.

THE SAXON HOUSE OF WETTIN

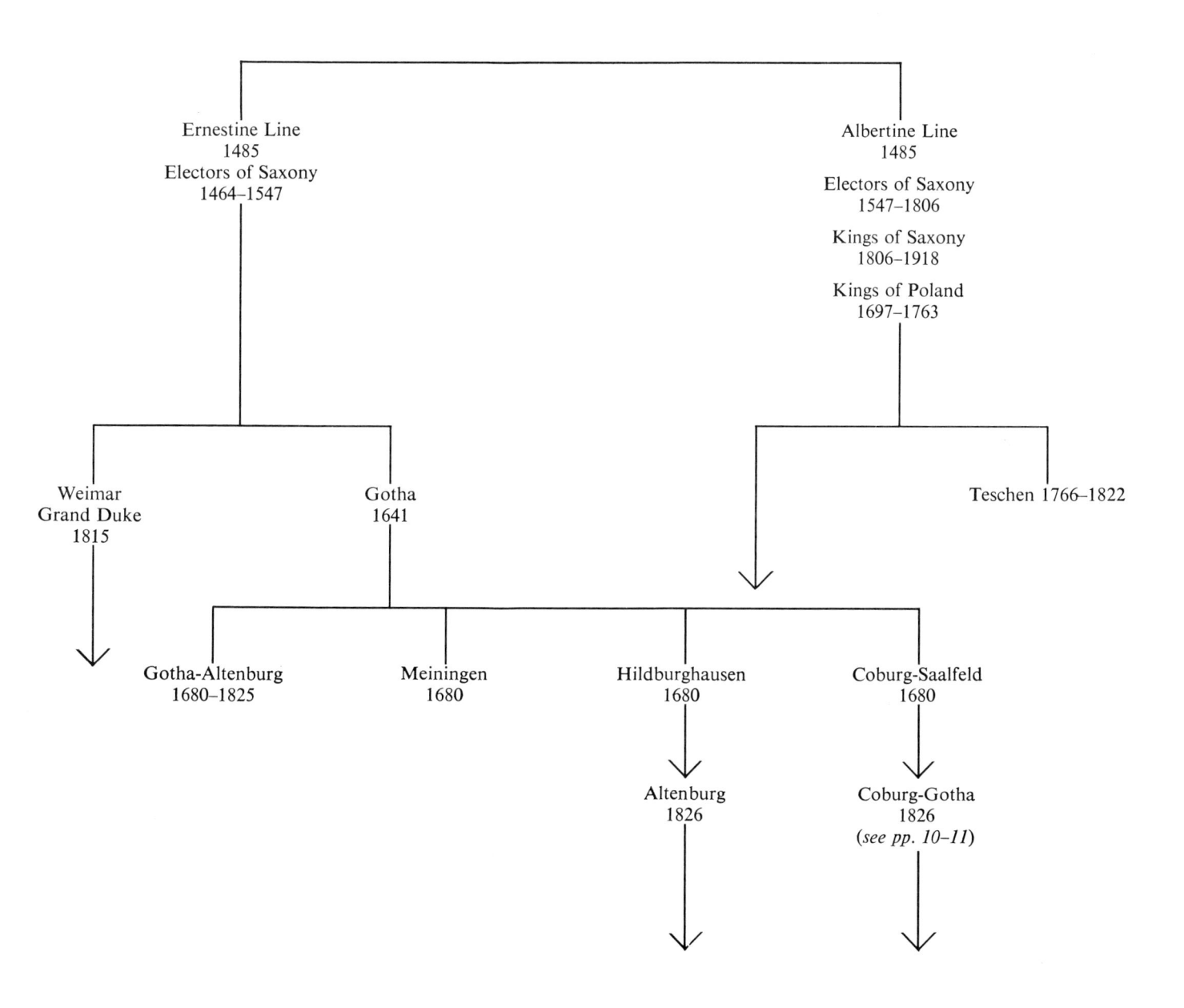

```
                                    |
        ┌───────────────────────────┴───────────────────────────┐
   Ernestine Line                                         Albertine Line
       1485                                                   1485
  Electors of Saxony                                    Electors of Saxony
     1464–1547                                              1547–1806

                                                         Kings of Saxony
                                                            1806–1918

                                                         Kings of Poland
                                                            1697–1763

   ┌──────────┴──────────┐                              ┌─────────┴─────────┐
 Weimar                Gotha                                            Teschen 1766–1822
 Grand Duke            1641
   1815
                         │
                         ▼
   ┌──────────┬──────────┼──────────┬──────────┐
Gotha-Altenburg    Meiningen   Hildburghausen   Coburg-Saalfeld
  1680–1825         1680          1680              1680
                                    │                 │
                                    ▼                 ▼
                                Altenburg         Coburg-Gotha
                                  1826               1826
                                                 (see pp. 10–11)
```

Albert: the Grooming Years 33

(below)
Ernest I, Duke of Saxe-Coburg-Gotha (1784–1844)
Miniature by W. Schmidt (Royal Collection)

Ernest I succeeded his father as Duke of Coburg in a moment of extreme adversity after the Prussian defeat at Jena in 1806. The Tsar's intervention saved the duchy from confiscation by Napoleon, to whom the new Duke had to pay court at Paris. From there he brought back as mistress Pauline Panam, 'la belle grecque', whose later account of her adventures was to prove so harmful to him. By his marriage to Louise of Saxe-Gotha he had two sons, Ernest and Albert.

Almost alone among Germany's sovereign princes, with Karl August, Duke of Saxe-Weimar, Ernest I fulfilled the promise to grant a constitution to his state in 1821, and he reorganized the administration and finances of the duchy very ably. In 1826 he acquired the duchy of Gotha on the extinction of its line of dukes and in the same year divorced his wife, marrying after her death Marie of Württemberg, who survived him.

As a youth he was preferable to his brothers Ferdinand and Leopold, according to Caroline Bauer, lighthearted and often lightminded but always frank and happy. He took a keen interest in the education and upbringing of his sons and always enjoyed their company. 'My father joined to his rare personal beauty a mind evenly balanced in every way and a deep inward calm... my father was at home in many branches of science, and had, as was necessary in his duties as regent, become a farseeing and sharpwitted man of business,' wrote Duke Ernest II in his memoirs. He continued, 'What won all hearts was the earnest mildness with which he interested himself in everything... I never heard a harsh or ugly word from his lips, never saw an action of his which would not have satisfied every idea of good breeding.'

(bottom right)
Louise of Saxe-Gotha, Duchess of Saxe-Coburg (1800–1831)
Anonymous miniature (Royal Collection)

The last scion of the Dukes of Saxe-Gotha, Louise married Ernest I, Duke of Saxe-Coburg, when she was seventeen. He was twice her age. At first she was supremely happy and enchanted with Coburg and Rosenau. In June 1818 her elder son Ernest was born, followed, on 26 August 1819, by Albert, in each case with the professional assistance of Dr. Charlotte von Siebold.

After this the marriage became unhappy, whether due to the revelations of the Duke's former mistress, Madame Panam, published in 1823 or to the Duke's relationship with Colonel von Szymborski remains unclear, while the Duchess was increasingly attracted to Alexander von Hanstein, a young Coburg officer. In August 1824 Szymborski proposed to her a partial separation from the Duke. When the people of the duchy heard this they went to Rosenau and dragged her carriage back to Coburg, but despite this forced reunion with the Duke and her sons, Duchess Louise signed a deed of separation and left Coburg for ever. 'Parting from my children was the worst thing of all.' The Duchess went to St. Wendel in the Coburgs' Rhenish principality of Lichtenberg and after a divorce in 1826 married Hanstein.

Caroline Bauer described her as an 'elegant attractive woman with fair locks and blue eyes'. She may have been on occasion flighty and emptyheaded, but she proved generally popular with all classes. When she dined at Rodach en route to Coburg after her wedding, Superintendent Hohnbaum wrote of her, 'She is an extremely natural and amiable creature. In Coburg, however, they will keep her in the polishing mill and under the roller till she turns out smooth and even like the rest. Altogether it is my belief that no idle words can ever have desecrated her lips nor any court vice have corrupted her heart. In my eyes she is an extraordinarily rare creature.' Stockmar remembered Duchess Louise with her sad, pretty face and when he accompanied Albert to Italy he found in him 'a striking resemblance to his mother', both physically and mentally, 'the same nobility and readiness of mind, the same intelligence, the same overruling desire and talent for appearing kind and amiable to others'.

Queen Victoria, who disapproved strongly of divorced women, wrote later, 'the Prince never forgot her, and spoke with much tenderness of his poor mother, and was deeply affected in reading, after his marriage, the accounts of her sad and painful illness.' The Queen described her as 'full of cleverness and talent' and named her fourth daughter after her. In consequence of the Duchess's separation from her husband, her rights of possession over the allodium of Gotha descended to her two sons, so that Prince Albert also enjoyed certain property rights there.

(opposite)
Queen Victoria, Prince Albert and their Five Eldest Children
Painting by Franz Xaver Winterhalter, 1846 (Royal Collection) *see chapter four*

Although portraits of royal families constitute a rich tradition in the history of court painting, few pictures succeed as well as Winterhalter's in capturing both the public and the private images of the popular, nineteenth-century monarchy. Prince Albert, wearing the Garter, sits next to the enthroned Queen, her arm around her heir, the Prince of Wales, whose position standing next to the throne emphasizes the allusion to dynastic continuity. The curtain gathered back to frame the composition is another traditional feature of official portraits, and the configuration of the drapery, especially the fold of the cloth filling the space between the head of the Queen and that of her husband, is remarkably close to that in Hyacinth Rigaud's celebrated *Portrait of Louis XIV* (Versailles), the prototype for many state portraits in the eighteenth and nineteenth centuries. These public trappings, however, are mixed quite freely with more domestic elements, especially the four children in the foreground, perhaps reflecting the less distant, more comfortable image of monarchy in the Victorian age. Even here Winterhalter drew on the work of earlier artists, and it is possible that Zoffany's intimate views of George III and his family were a general inspiration for this type of Royal Family group. The portrait of the young Prince Alfred, toddling across the picture plane, is reminiscent of the position and stance of the infant duc de Bretagne in Nicolas de Largillière's depiction of four generations of astonishingly relaxed Bourbons, *Louis XIV and his Heirs* (London, Wallace Collection), while the grouping of the Princess Royal and Princess Alice around the baby Princess Helena under a still-life of fruit and leaves, perhaps the most intimate and successful part of the canvas, seems to look back to a composition in a painting of almost identical subject, *The Five Children of Charles I* (Royal Collection), by one of the greatest court portraitists, Anthony van Dyck. Winterhalter's unique skill in grouping several figures, apparent in *Florinda* (see p. 65) and *The Empress Eugénie and her Ladies* (Compiègne, Musée National), is paramount here, and the meticulous handling of the still-lifes, the lively rendering of light falling on fabric and the almost Impressionistic shreds and dabs of colour defining the pattern of the carpet all tend to rebut Winterhalter's unearned reputation as an insipid society artist and a dead colourist. This painting originally hung in the dining-room at Osborne. It was removed to Buckingham Palace in 1901, and a copy substituted for it at Osborne.

34 Albert: the Grooming Years

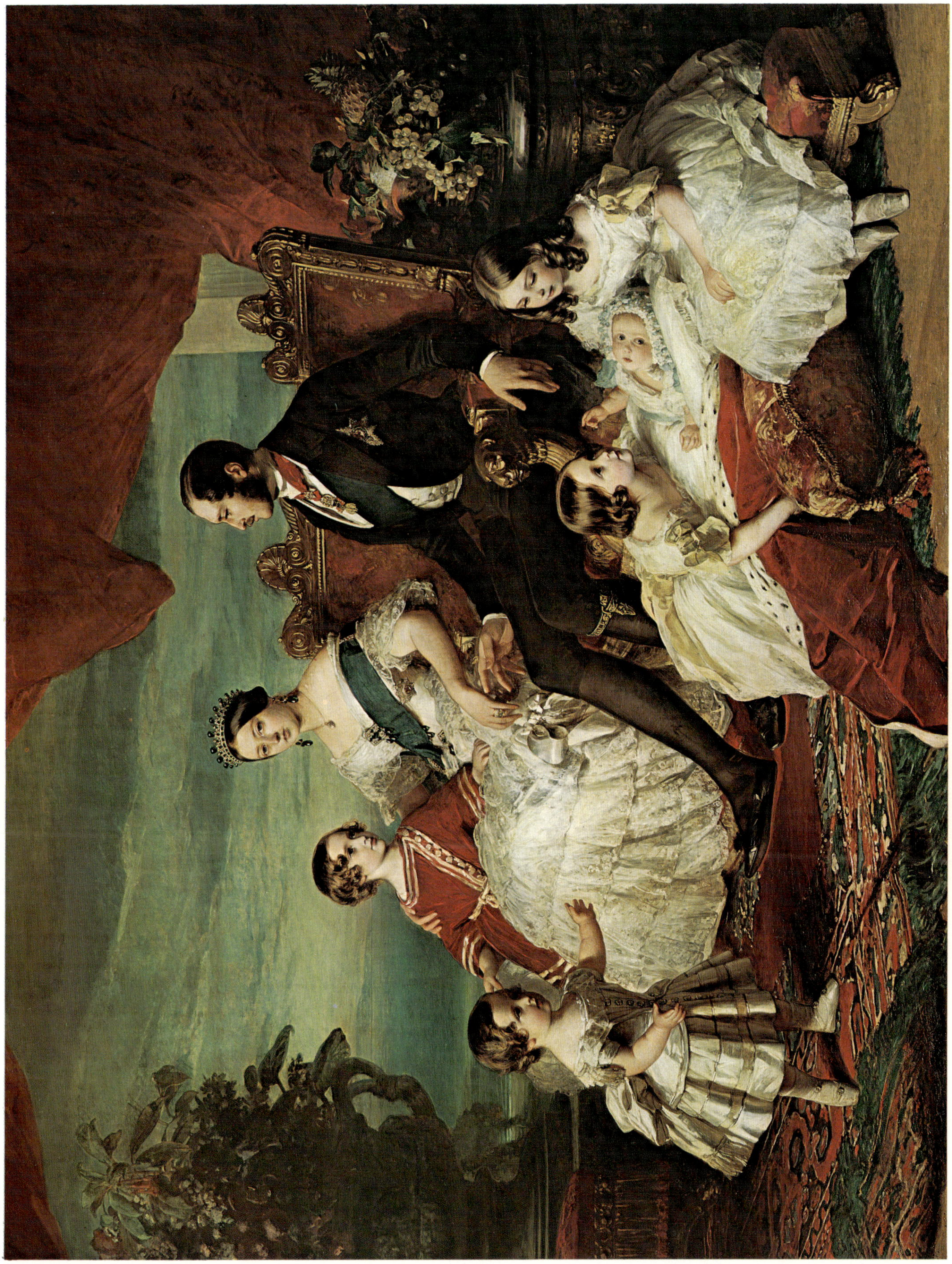

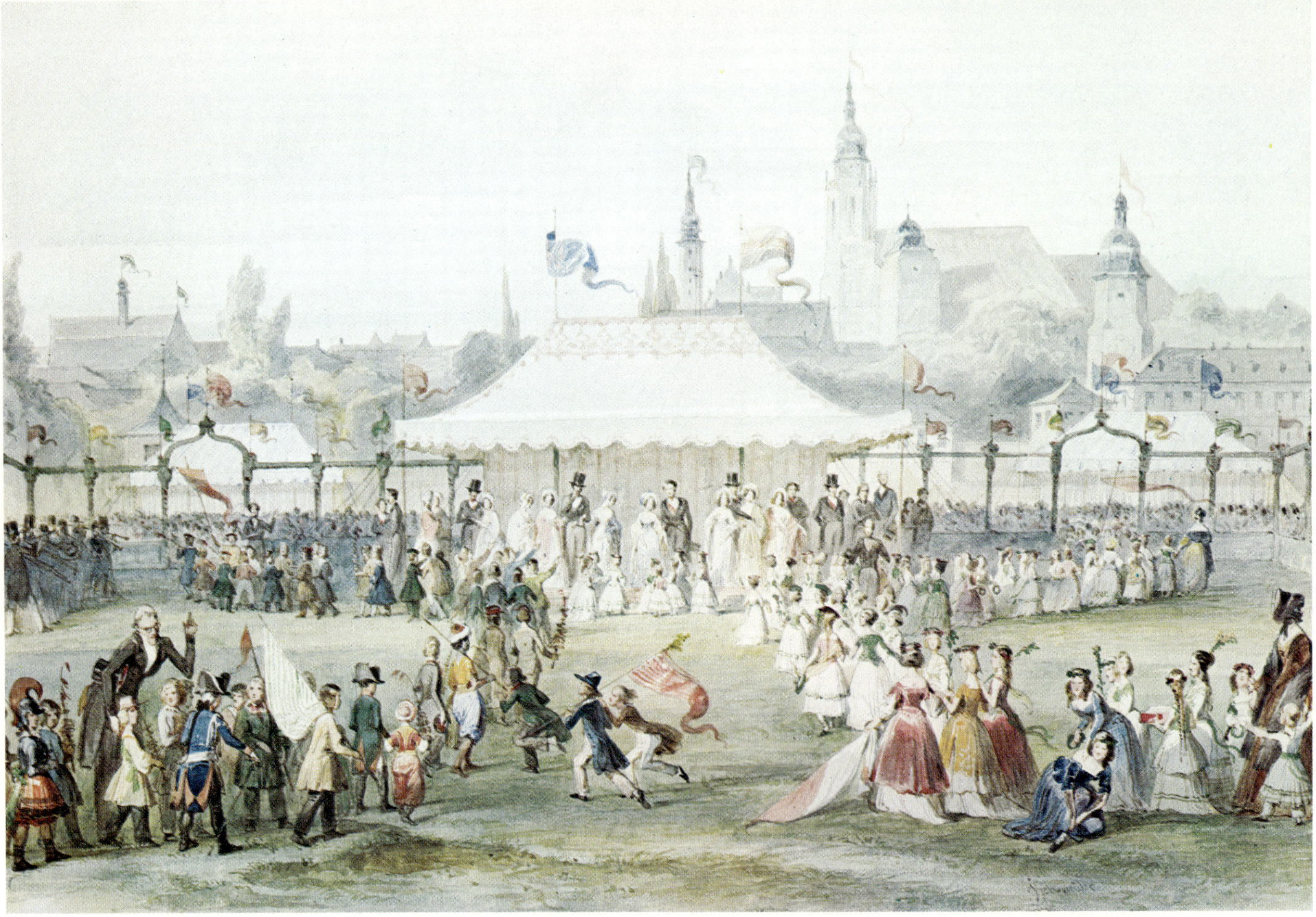

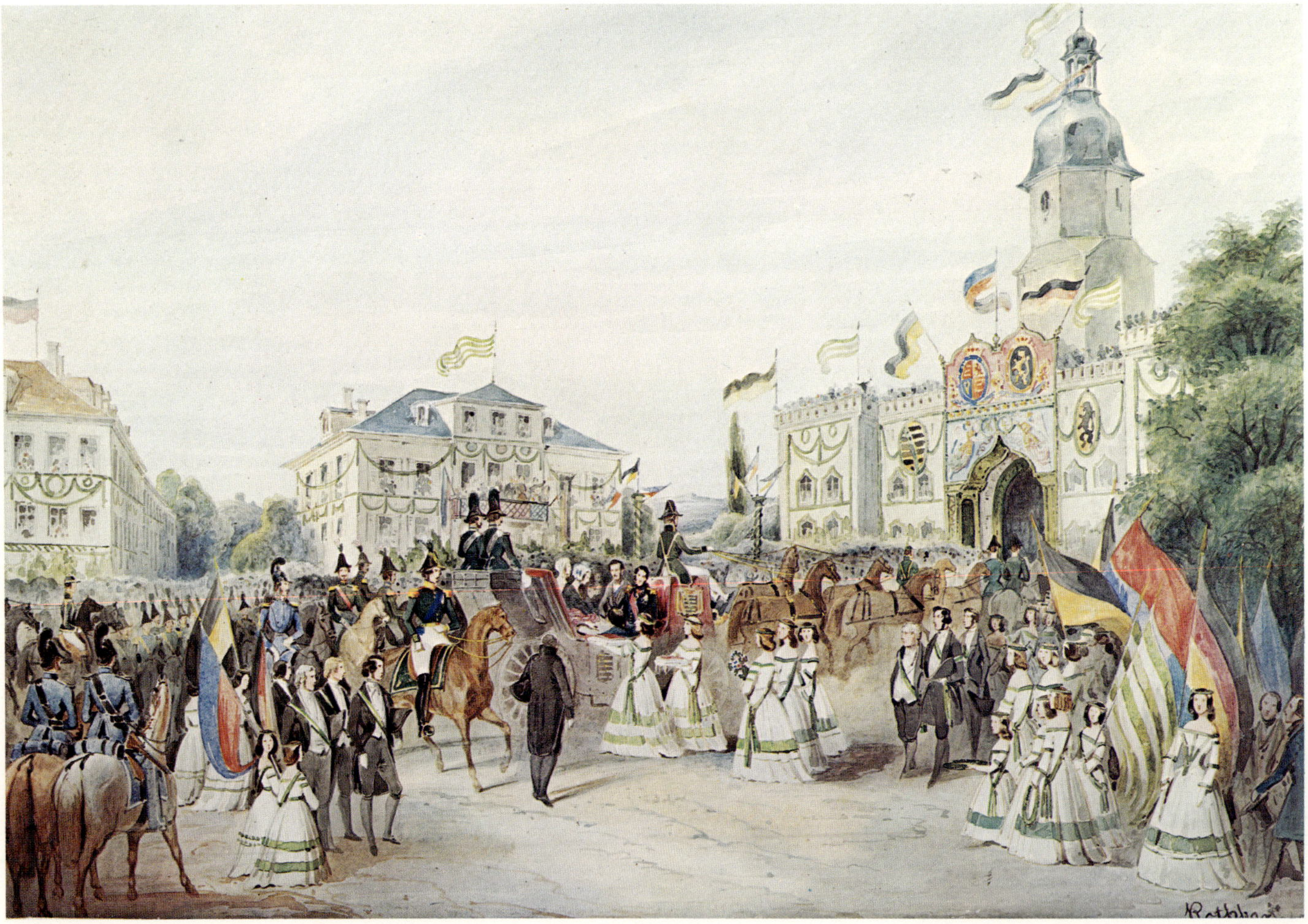

Caroline Amelia of Hesse-Kassel, Duchess of Saxe-Gotha (1771–1848)
Engraving by Franz Hanfstängel (British Museum)

'Dear good Grandmama. She was an angel upon Earth, and to us ever so good and loving,' Prince Albert wrote to his stepmother on the Duchess of Gotha's death, which he felt severely. In 1845 the Queen met her and described her as 'a charming old lady and though very small, remarkably nice-looking, erect and active; but unfortunately very deaf.'

The second wife of Augustus, Duke of Saxe-Gotha, she had no children but was a most affectionate step-mother to his only daughter Louise, Duchess of Saxe-Coburg, and a doting grandmother to her stepdaughter's motherless sons Ernest and Albert, who often stayed with Duchess Caroline at Gotha. Stockmar wrote to Prince Albert of her 'upright and honourable nature and her truly motherly love for yourself' (7 May 1841).

Although she never visited England, the Duchess was closely related to its Royal Family, her father being a grandson of George II and her father-in-law a nephew of Augusta, Princess of Wales, both Knights of the Garter. This led her to appreciate keenly its conferment on Ernest I of Saxe-Coburg on Queen Victoria's coronation.

(*opposite top*)
Festival on the 'Anger' at Coburg, 22 August 1845
Watercolour by Heinrich Schneider (Royal Collection) *see chapter four*

The 'Anger', or Common, was a scene of popular festivals at Coburg, redolent of its patriarchal conditions. No family festival at court was considered complete without popular representation, nor popular festivals without the presence of the ducal family. Prince Albert therefore wrote to his brother (28 June 1845), 'What I think would give Victoria a great deal of pleasure would be to see the children's festival, and a dinner in the Anger would be something perfectly new and characteristic of Coburg. All the peasants from the country who come to Coburg on such occasions and their various costumes would interest Victoria.'

22 August, the Feast of St. Gregory, was the occasion for the annual children's festival. From the palace balcony the Queen watched 1300 schoolchildren march into the courtyard to sing *God Save the Queen*. 'After this we drove to the Anger, a meadow close to the town. Here were pitched two tents, decorated with flowers, and open at the sides under which we were to dine. All the children were in front of us. We walked round among them and then sat down to dinner. A band of music played the whole time... the children danced... and they played games, and were so truly happy—the evening was so beautiful—the whole scene so animated—the good people so quiet, it was the prettiest thing I ever saw,' the Queen recorded in her journal.

It was an idyllic picture of the Biedermeier Germany preceding the Revolution of March 1848, the Age of Railways and of unification by 'Blood and Iron'. Instead this was the age of idealism from which Prince Albert stemmed.

(*opposite bottom*)
The Entry of Queen Victoria and Prince Albert into Coburg, 19 August 1845
Watercolour by F. Rothbart (Royal Collection) *see chapter four*

The Queen and Prince Albert travelled by carriage from Mainz to Coburg. They were met at the frontier with its triumphal arch by Duke Ernest and a crowd in local dress.

'We then drove to Ketschendorf, the pretty little house of our dear late grandmother, where we found Uncle Leopold and Louise who got into the carriage with us. Ernest mounted a horse and rode next to the carriage on my side... Then the procession was formed, which looked extremely pretty. At the entrance to the town, we came to another triumphal arch where Herr Bergner, the Burgomaster, addressed us and was quite overcome. On the other side stood a number of young girls dressed in white, with green wreaths and scarfs, who presented us with bouquets and verses. I cannot say how much I felt moved on entering this dear old place and with difficulty I restrained my emotion. The beautifully ornamented town, all bright with wreaths and the numbers of good affectionate people, the many recollections connected with the place—all was so affecting. In the Platz... the clergy were assembled, and Ober-Superintendent Genzler addressed us very kindly.'

Thus the Queen described in her journal their entry into Coburg, the Prince's first homecoming since his marriage. The scene was decorated in green and white, the colours of the duchy, the British red, white and blue, and the red, gold and black of Belgium, also the colours of the German national unity movement, as today of the German Federal Republic. The Duchess of Kent was waiting at the Ehrenburg Palace and no less than sixty-one persons of royal, imperial or princely families were expected to greet the royal visitors.

Albert: the Grooming Years 37

Ernest II, Duke of Saxe-Coburg-Gotha (1818–1893)
Miniature by Sir William Ross (Royal Collection)

In his memoirs Duke Ernest wrote of the uniquely close bond of intimacy with his brother Albert. They were never separated until 1839 when Albert went to Italy and Ernest, like many of the Coburg nobility, received military training in Saxony. Henceforward their paths diverged, but they were alike in seeking a united constitutional Germany. Ernest's continual financial difficulties and moral laxity, however, were a constant source of severe disquiet to Prince Albert.

Ernest II, who succeeded his father in 1844, was the only German ruler to take part in the 1848 campaign in Schleswig-Holstein against the Danes, and he supported Prussia in 1849–50. In the subsequent decade of reaction he did not withdraw constitutional concessions made in 1848 and offered asylum to the protagonists of national and liberal ideas, as also to the Duke of Augustenburg, the German claimant to Schleswig-Holstein. He gave patronage to the choral, gymnastic and shooting concourses which brought together Germans from all states and so fostered the national idea, earning the sobriquet 'Schützenherzog' ('Marksman Duke') to the disquiet of his fellow princes. He also became protector in 1859 of the National Verein for union under Prussian leadership, which had its headquarters at Coburg. His military convention with Prussia in 1861 placed the Coburg and Gotha forces under Prussian command, with notable consequences for Hanover in 1866, and he was proud of the rank he thus acquired as a Prussian general. He had earned his mead of gratitude from the newly proclaimed Emperor William I at Versailles in 1871, 'I do not forget that I have to thank your efforts in great part for the main essence of this day.'

The Duke was the first foreign prince to visit Paris under the Second Empire in March 1854, thus preparing the way for the Queen and Prince Albert. Thanks to the assistance of Napoleon III and of Meyerbeer, his opera *Santa Chiara* was presented in Paris (24 September 1855). Ernest II left no legitimate offspring and was succeeded as Duke of Saxe-Coburg, as Prince Albert had planned, by his and the Queen's second son, Alfred, Duke of Edinburgh.

Augusta of Reuss-Ebersdorf, Duchess of Saxe-Coburg (1757–1831)
Anonymous miniature (Royal Collection)

'She was a most remarkable woman, with a most powerful, energetic, almost masculine mind, accompanied with great tenderness of heart and extreme love for Nature... She was adored by her children, particularly by her sons, King Leopold being her great favourite. She had fine and most expressive blue eyes, with the marked features and long nose inherited by most of her children and grandchildren. Both the Prince and his brother were exceedingly attached to her and they lived much with her in their younger days,' Queen Victoria recollected in *The Early Years of the Prince Consort*.

Augusta was a daughter of the Count of Reuss-Ebersdorf, a family in which all males bore the name of Henry and as counts were inferior in rank to the ducal houses of Saxony. Through her Prince Albert had many relatives of noble but not princely rank. She married Francis, Duke of Saxe-Coburg-Saalfeld in 1777, when the Emperor had installed a Debt and Administrative Commission or receivership because of the virtual bankruptcy of the duchy of Coburg. Duchess Augusta's parents were 'Herrnhuter'. Her father's aunt Erdmutha Dorothea had married Nicholas Ludwig, Graf von Zinzendorf, on whose estate at Herrnhut the Moravians found sanctuary and organized their community of Brethren. They spread their missionary activity from there to all continents, while Countess Erdmutha, who administered the estate in her husband's frequent missionary absences, also composed hymns. This background accounted for Duchess Augusta's strong piety and resignation to God's will, and also for her extremely strict, often narrow, moral views which she imparted in large measure, like her physical features, to Prince Albert. Her experiences in the Napoleonic period imbued her with strong anti-French resentments. She gave expression to these in her attitude to Madame Panam, Ernest I's French mistress of Greek origin, with disastrous results for him.

The Duchess, widowed in 1806, lived at Ketschendorf near Coburg. She visited her son Leopold at Claremont in 1825. Queen Victoria met her then and remembered her grandmother clearly.

(*opposite*)
Frederick the Wise, Elector of Saxony (1463–1525)
Etching by Prince Albert after a painting by Lucas Cranach (British Museum)

In 1485 the lands of the House of Wettin, rulers of Saxony, one of the seven electorates of the Holy Roman Empire, were divided between the two sons of Frederick the Gentle, Ernest and Albert, thus creating the Ernestine (or electoral) and Albertine lines of the family (*see p. 33*). In their boyhood the two brothers were the victims of a kidnapping plot, happily frustrated by a charcoal burner, a favourite story of Prince Albert in childhood.

The Elector Ernest's son and successor, Frederick the Wise, became the patron and protector of Martin Luther, who, disguised as Junker Jörg, translated the New Testament in the electoral castle of the Wartburg. The Imperial election of 1519, which resulted in the choice of the Spanish Charles V as Holy Roman Emperor, ushered in an almost unbroken line of Catholic Habsburg Holy Roman Emperors. Many German princes would have welcomed the elevation of Frederick the Wise to the Imperial dignity, but the Saxon elector felt that the family division of the Wettin lands with their mineral wealth left the Ernestine branch with an insufficient power base. Frederick's immediate successors as Electors of Saxony continued the Ernestine policy of support for the Reformation, for which they suffered in 1546 when the victorious Charles V transferred the electoral title to their Albertine cousins. The Ernestine lands were subsequently subdivided and ducal dynasties established at Weimar, Meiningen, Coburg and Gotha, the last two lines being the direct ancestors of Prince Albert. The memory of the loss of the electorate and other sufferings for the Protestant cause survived in the Ernestine House of Saxe-Coburg down to the nineteenth century. The Albertine line became Catholic after Augustus the Strong was elected King of Poland in 1697.

Prince Albert was an avid admirer of Lucas Cranach, a friend of Luther, and bought more pictures by him than by any other painter, except Winterhalter and Landseer, including one of Luther as Junker Jörg. Prince Albert etched this portrait of Frederick the Wise, dated 1 December 1840, after Cranach's painting, dated 1532, which he had acquired in 1840.

38 *Albert: the Grooming Years*

Albert: the Grooming Years 39

40 Albert: the Grooming Years

(*opposite top*)
Rosenau: the Marmorsaal
Watercolour by Ferdinand Rothbart (Royal Collection)

The grey and gilt Marble Hall is the ballroom of Rosenau. Its white marble sheathing gives a luminosity to offset its subterranean qualities. Situated on the lowest level of the building it opens on to the garden with most pleasant views over meadows, stream and wooded hills. Here Prince Albert was christened on 19 September 1819.

(*opposite bottom*)
Rosenau: the Room occupied by Princes Ernest and Albert as boys
Watercolour by Ferdinand Rothbart (Royal Collection)

The room 'where my dearest Albert and Ernest used to live. It is quite in the roof, with a tiny little bedroom on each side, in one of which they both used to sleep with Florschütz their tutor. The view is beautiful. . . and the very same table is there on which they were dressed when little.' This description by Queen Victoria summarizes perfectly the bare, simple circumstances in which the boys were reared.

Gotha with the Castle of Friedenstein
Watercolour by H. Brueckner (Royal Collection)

Gotha was the capital of the duchy of Saxe-Gotha, the home of Prince Albert's mother as also of King George III's mother, Augusta, Princess of Wales. It is situated on the north side of the Thüringer Wald, or Thuringian Forest, and is now in the German Democratic Republic. The town is dominated by the ducal residence, Schloss Friedenstein (built 1643–54), on the right of this watercolour. The castle houses a magnificent collection of incunabula, manuscripts, coins and medals, pictures, engravings and orientalia built up by the Dukes of Gotha. Here Duchess Louise was born in 1800 and here she was married in 1817 to Ernest I, Duke of Coburg.

In the eighteenth century the Dukes of Gotha made their capital a centre of French culture, and it was in close touch with the Weimar of Goethe and Schiller. The *Almanach de Gotha* from 1763 on gave genealogical details of reigning families, while the Geographische Anstalt of Justus Perthes, founded in 1785, was a pioneer in modern cartography. The first German commercial academy was founded at Gotha in 1812.

(*opposite top*)
Reinhardsbrunn
Watercolour by Heinrich Schneider, 1840 (Royal Collection)

The country house of Reinhardsbrunn was built (1827–35) by Duke Ernest I in his newly acquired duchy of Gotha, on the site of a Benedictine monastery destroyed in the Peasants War in 1525. Surrounded by a magnificent park, it contains a fine collection of antlers and antler furniture and gave more pleasure to Queen Victoria than any residence except Rosenau. Reinhardsbrunn is situated near Friedrichsroda, a popular resort on the edge of the Thüringer Wald. Ernest I had paths built to its finest beauty spots, thus attracting many tourists.

(*opposite bottom*)
Ehrenburg Palace, Coburg
Watercolour, 1846 (Royal Collection)

In 1547 the Duke of Coburg built a Renaissance-style residence on the site of the suppressed Franciscan monastery at the edge of the town. Although the edifice was largely rebuilt by Duke Ernest I in English Gothic style, the remarkable 'Riesensaal' of 1690, named after the giant figures which support the ceiling, was preserved. On the right of the watercolour stands the late Gothic Moritzkirche, in which Luther preached, the court theatre on the extreme right and the Hauptwache on the left. Beyond the Hauptwache lies the Hofgarten, containing the mausoleum of Prince Albert's paternal grandparents, Duke Francis and Duchess Augusta, and the Natural History Museum, which includes the boyhood collections of Prince Albert and his brother.

Friedrichsthal
Watercolour, 1842 (Royal Collection)

The palace of Friedrichsthal was built in 1712 on the outskirts of Gotha. It became the summer residence of the Dowager Duchess Caroline Amelia. Here she was often visited by her grandsons Ernest and Albert. Queen Victoria and Prince Albert stayed with her here in 1845.

Albert: the Grooming Years 43

Princes Ernest and Albert of Saxe-Coburg
Painting by Leopold Döll (Royal Collection)

This picture of the two Princes, Albert on the left and Ernest on the right, feeding a pet rabbit, was painted when they were aged four and five respectively, just after Florschütz took them over from their nurse to the dismay of their Gotha grandmother. 'Brought up together', the tutor reported, 'they went hand in hand in all things, whether at work or at play. Engaging in the same pursuits, sharing the same joys and the same sorrows, they were bound to each other by no common feelings of mutual love.' This was some months before their mother left them and Coburg forever in September 1824.

Caroline Bauer spoke of 'the altogether lovely blond-locked Prince Albert whose whole figure savoured of the angelic'. He was his mother's favourite, and Stockmar observed years later that he 'bears a striking resemblance to his mother, and at the same time, though differing much, takes after her in many respects, both physical and mental. He has the same nobility and readiness of mind, the same intelligence, the same overruling desire and talent for appearing amiable and kind to others, the same tendency to espièglerie.'

Leopold Döll (d. 1856) was court painter and curator of casts of ancient statues at Gotha. He came from a family of artists. His father had been sent by Ernest II, Duke of Gotha, the Princes' great-grandfather and a patron of artists, including Tischbein, to study in Paris and Rome, following which he was placed in charge of the artistic treasures of Gotha. The original painting is at Gotha and was specially hung in Queen Victoria's bedroom at Friedrichsthal in 1845.

Medal
Issued to Commemorate the Confirmation of Princes Ernest and Albert of Saxe-Coburg-Gotha, 12 April 1835 (British Museum)

The obverse shows the two Princes, Ernest to the left, Albert to the right. On 11 April the two brothers were publicly examined in religious knowledge in the 'Riesensaal' of Ehrenburg Palace in Coburg by the court chaplain Dr. Jacobi in the presence of the Duke of Coburg, the Dowager Duchess of Gotha and five other Serene Highnesses. The household, heads of government departments and deputations from the Diet, the clergy, the towns and villages attended, the Duke regarding himself as the head of the great family of his subjects. The examination lasted an hour, and the Princes' clear answers, no mere 'yes' or 'no', showed deep feeling and inward conviction and testified to their encyclopedic preparation. In their religious formation the Princes were much influenced by the 'Rational Supernaturalism' of Dr. K. G. Bretschneider, General Superintendent of Gotha, who was a friend of the ducal family and emphasized the ethical content of Christianity rather than divisive dogmatism.

On the following day, Palm Sunday, Ernest and Albert were solemnly confirmed in the palace chapel by Dr. Genzler, General Superintendent of Coburg, who had christened them and had married the Duke and Duchess of Kent. After this the court drove to the Moritzkirche, which was packed with thousands, for a special service of thanksgiving.

On 13 April a grand banquet took place in the 'Riesensaal'. Duke Ernest bestowed numerous marks of favour on those who had taken part in the Princes' education, while the town of Coburg presented their tutor, Councillor Florschütz, who was later to marry the daughter of Superintendent Genzler, with a diamond ring. The Duke had invited many representatives of Gotha for the occasion and they were most kindly entertained by the Coburgers.

44 Albert: the Grooming Years

Christian Friedrich, Baron von Stockmar (1787–1863)
Painting by Franz Xaver Winterhalter, 1847 (Royal Collection)

Stockmar was a Coburger whose wealthy grandfather repeatedly made loans to the impecunious Duke which were never repaid. Medical training gave him a capacity for diagnosis, often theoretical rather than pragmatic, which he employed on the diplomatic scene. He went to London as personal physician to Prince Leopold, who called him 'dearest soul and body doctor'. When Princess Charlotte died, Leopold, heartbroken, kissed her cold hand and turned to Stockmar with the words 'I am now quite forsaken; promise me to keep ever by me.' He became Leopold's constant adviser, receiving a Saxon patent of nobility in 1821. He assisted the Prince in his quest for the Greek and Belgian crowns and, above all, in his scheme for the marriage of Queen Victoria to Prince Albert, whom he accompanied to Italy in 1839. It was Stockmar who was entrusted with the negotiation of the marriage contract for Albert.

His cousin Caroline Bauer described him in 1822 as being 'no beauty, but of a fine, slim, superior appearance, showing somewhat Anglified manners; with eyes expressive of lively sagacity and which looked at me very penetratingly as though they would probe into my most secret thoughts. His genially pleasing and winning smile was not seldom dashed by a bitter flavour, giving decided token of ascendancy, of satire or irony.' She found him a grating mixture of German and English, citizen and courtier. Ambition and love of power motivated his actions. He married a cousin with a fortune of 100,000 thalers 'for the sake of being able to hold a perfectly independent footing in relation to Prince Leopold. He felt that his power rested on this independence.' Stockmar loved Leopold 'whom he ruled by his intellectual superiority'. His wife was left to ossify in Coburg into 'personified avarice, and by this avarice revenged herself, latterly, in a dreadful manner on her poor old dying husband,' wrote Caroline Bauer.

For many years he usually spent the winter in England, having rooms set apart for him at Buckingham Palace, Windsor and Osborne. He was privileged to wear trousers instead of knee breeches at the Queen's table as he had thin legs and suffered from chills—he was a great hypochondriac. Each spring he disappeared suddenly, hating to take leave, and he never returned after 1857. Stockmar took an active part in the events of 1848–49 in Germany, representing Coburg in the Frankfurt and Erfurt Parliaments, and even aspired to be German Prime Minister with Bunsen as Foreign Secretary. Failing in this project, he successfully supported Charles of Leiningen for the post, and thenceforward his interests centred in Germany. Stockmar's son Ernest became private secretary to the Princess Royal in Berlin in 1858.

The death of Prince Albert was a bitter blow; he had loved him like a son. Stockmar's tombstone in the Coburg cemetery testifies to the reciprocation of this devotion; it is inscribed, 'To the memory of Baron von Stockmar from his friends in the ruling families of Belgium, Coburg, England and Prussia. There is a friend that adheres closer than a brother.'

Albert: the Grooming Years

Vue de Bonn

46 Albert: the Grooming Years

(*opposite*)
Laeken
Watercolour by J. Fourmois (Royal Collection)

The palace of Laeken outside Brussels was built 1782-84 by Montoyer and Payen in Louis XVI style for Albert, Duke of Saxe-Teschen, Governor of the Austrian Netherlands and husband to a sister of Queen Marie Antoinette. Shortly before his death in 1822, the Duke became one of Prince Albert's godfathers. Sacked by the French Revolutionary army in 1792, the palace was restored by Napoleon, who is said to have planned his Russian campaign there.

Laeken is linked to Brussels by the Allée Verte, along which Belgium's rulers traditionally made their *joyeuse entrée* into the capital, a custom observed in 1831 by King Leopold I following Belgium's establishment as an independent kingdom. Leopold made Laeken the royal residence and was visited there in 1832 by his nephews Ernest and Albert. In 1836 they returned to Brussels for a longer stay, living in a villa in the Boulevard de l'Observation.

(*below*)
Bonn from the River
Panoramic view by Charles Gore, 1790 (British Museum)

Gore, an amateur watercolourist and marine draughtsman, was born in 1729. He was a Lincolnshire landowner with an inborn love of the sea and shipping. On account of the health of his wife, a Yorkshire heiress, he left England in 1773 to winter in Lisbon. In 1774 he secured a passage in a British frigate to convey him and his family to Italy by way of Gibraltar and Minorca. He visited, among other places, Rome, Naples and Florence, where in 1775 his youngest daughter, Anne, was married to George, third Earl Cowper. Their second son, the fifth earl, married Lord Melbourne's sister, Emily, who, after her husband's death, became the wife of Viscount Palmerston. Gore spent April and May 1779 in Sicily in the company of the antiquary Richard Payne Knight and the German artist Jakob Philipp Hackert, court painter to Ferdinand IV of Naples and a close personal friend of Goethe. Gore, too, established a firm friendship with Goethe, being the only Englishman to enjoy this privilege.

After a spell in England and Florence, Gore settled permanently in Weimar in 1791 and remained there as a member of the ducal court until his death in 1807. According to his wish, five large folios of his drawings were handed over to Duke Karl August and are now in the Thüringische Landesbibliothek in Weimar.

Albert: the Grooming Years 47

(opposite)
Friedrich von Schiller (1759–1805)
Lithograph by C. Unte, printed for the poet's centenary, 1859 (British Museum)

A south German, Schiller became Professor of History at the Ernestine University of Jena in 1789. Here he came into closer contact with Goethe and the literary circle of Weimar, where he settled in 1799. During these years he wrote his dramatic trilogy *Wallenstein,* centring on the man who, in the Thirty Years War, sought by means of his army to become the chief power in Germany and to transcend the divisions of religion. His drama *Wilhelm Tell* (1804) glorified the Swiss struggle for constitutionalism and independence.

In 1799 Schiller also completed his greatest non-dramatic poem *Das Lied von der Glocke*, describing the founding of a bell with its motto 'Vivos voco, Mortuos plango, Fulgura frango'. Hoisted into the tower it rings the message of peace to men, 'Concordia'. The bell reflects the changing play of life with its joys and sorrows. *The Song of the Bell*, an English version, was included in the programme of music at Windsor Castle, 10 February 1853, the thirteenth anniversary of the Queen's marriage. The words of the chorus foreshadow strongly Prince Albert's views:

When labour is by art directed,
The work it robs of half its toil ...

With sober aim to serious end,
Be skill and industry combined;
Man's work must ever end in failure,
Unless it bear the stamp of mind.

The late eighteenth-century literary revival, fostered by the influence of Protestant England, had given the Germans a sense of national consciousness, which received an immense impetus from the struggle against Napoleonic France. The younger generation of Germans, including the two Coburg Princes, steeped in Romanticism, therefore acclaimed Schiller as Germany's national poet.

The centenary of his birth was celebrated by Germans throughout the world and, coinciding with the arousing of national feeling by the Franco-Austrian War of 1859, led to the founding of the National Verein, which helped to prepare German public opinion for national unity under Prussian leadership. Its motto 'Seid einig, einig, einig' ('Be united') was drawn from Schiller's *Wilhelm Tell*.

Prince Albert's Residence at Bonn
Watercolour by C. Hohe (Royal Collection)

On the advice of Carl von Savigny, Professor of Civil Law at Berlin and the protagonist of the Historicist doctrine of the evolution of political institutions, Ernest and Albert were sent to study at Bonn. Berlin University, which enjoyed immense academic prestige, was considered to have too many military distractions for young princes. In May 1837 the brothers entered the 'Rhenish Frederick William's University' of Bonn, which had been founded in 1817 by the city's new Hohenzollern sovereign as a joint Catholic-Evangelical University with separate denominational chairs in theology and history as a means of assimilating the predominantly Catholic Rhinelanders into the Prussian monarchy.

The Princes, with their tutor Florschütz, their governor Baron von Wichmann and a household of fifteen persons, rented this small but neat house, on one side of an open piece of ground near the Dom, from Dr. Bischof, Professor of Medicine. It was very quiet and enjoyed fine views of the Rhine, the Siebengebirge and the Kreuzberg, seen in the background.

48 Albert: the Grooming Years

Albert: the Grooming Years 49

Medal
Issued to Commemorate the Wedding of Queen Victoria and Prince Albert, 10 February 1840 (British Museum)

The Marriage of Queen Victoria and Prince Albert at the Chapel Royal, St. James's Palace, 10 February 1840
Painting by Sir George Hayter, 1842 (Royal Collection)

To the right of the Queen stands Lord Melbourne, holding the Sword of State. Immediately in front of the Archbishop of Canterbury is the Duke of Sussex and, behind the Archbishop, the Duchess of Kent, while on Prince Albert's right stand Queen Adelaide and the Duke of Saxe-Coburg. Prince Ernest of Saxe-Coburg is to the right of his father, as are the Duchess of Cambridge with Princess Mary Adelaide of Cambridge, later Duchess of Teck and mother of Queen Mary, and Prince George of Cambridge.

The wife of the American Minister in London was present at the ceremony and sent the following description to her niece, Sally Rutherford, on 19 February 1840. The Queen's dress 'was rich, beautiful, & in perfect taste. The train was held by twelve fair girls, daughters of the highest nobility, all in white, with orange flowers in their hair. The deportment of the royal bride was really beautiful. It blended the sensibility of the woman with the dignity of the Queen... The Prince is very handsome and graceful, and looks older than he is by several years.'

Albert and Victoria: the Golden Years

When the 'soi-disant prétendu', as the famous Whig hostess Lady Holland had described Prince Albert, assumed his position as the Queen's husband in 1840, he found himself at a great disadvantage, first, as a foreigner, and second, as the nephew of King Leopold of the Belgians. Already in 1836 the Prince had written to his step-mother from England, 'The climate of this country, the different way of living, and the late hours, do not agree with me.' Nor was he to find the attitude of many of the aristocracy, whose hedonistic scepticism and flexible morality contrasted so sharply with his own stringent code of ethics, any more congenial. Two major obstacles confronted him in the persons of Lord Melbourne, Prime Minister and Queen Victoria's unofficial 'father-confessor', and the Baroness Lehzen, who as a tenacious supporter of the House of Hanover was not prepared to accept displacement by a Coburg. Melbourne resigned in 1841, but Lehzen was not pensioned off until 1842. In addition, Prince Albert had to accept George Anson, who had formerly served Melbourne, as his private secretary. Apart from a few servants and a secretary to deal with German correspondence, there were no other Germans in the Prince's service. He yearned for Coburg. Writing to his brother in August 1840, he reflected sadly that, on his first birthday in England, his Swiss valet, Cart, and his beloved greyhound, Eos, were the only familiar faces. Nor was his financial position any more reassuring. In contrast to the £50,000 annuity enjoyed by Leopold at the time of his marriage to Princess Charlotte, and by the Queen Dowager, his own allowance was a mere £30,000, while his private resources were relatively meagre.

Tuned to concert pitch, Prince Albert found himself reduced to initiating necessary, if unpopular, reforms in the Queen's Household, thereby further exacerbating the formidable Lehzen, instead of playing the major rôle in the political affairs of the monarchy which Leopold and Stockmar had envisaged for him. There were compensations, however, not least being the bill of July 1840 which appointed him as sole regent until the majority of a successor, should the Queen, then pregnant, die. His patience was rewarded. Though Queen Victoria might remonstrate with King Leopold in January 1841 for desiring to see her as 'a delighted and delightful *maman au milieu d'une belle et nombreuse famille*', already by the following December, a month after the birth of the Prince of Wales, Anson noted that Her Majesty interested herself 'less and less about politics'. Prince Albert's ascendancy over the Queen had begun. In February 1852 the Queen wrote to King Leopold, 'Albert grows daily fonder and fonder of politics and business . . . and I grow daily to dislike them both more and more. We women are not *made* for governing.'

During the first two years of his marriage the one sure consolation Prince Albert could find was in music, the love and cultivation of which he had inherited from his ancestors. His grandfather, Augustus, Duke of Saxe-Gotha, himself a poet and composer, was the lifelong friend and patron of Carl Maria von Weber; his aunt, the Duchess of Kent, sang and composed waltzes and quicksteps for royal birthdays; his brother Ernest was a composer. Prince Albert was a talented performer on the piano, and, more especially, the organ, considering it 'the first of instruments'. On his second visit to Buckingham Palace in July 1842, Mendelssohn begged the Prince to play something for him on the organ. The composer wrote afterwards to his mother, 'He played a chorale by heart with the pedals—and so charmingly, precisely and accurately that it would have done credit to a professional.' Dissatisfied with the Queen's Private Band, which consisted entirely of wind instruments, Prince Albert transformed it into a string orchestra. He took a personal interest in the selection of music for concerts given by this band, which, at the Prince's instigation, gave the first performance in England of Schubert's 'Great' C Major Symphony.

From 1840 until they ceased in 1848, Prince Albert was a director of the Concerts of Ancient Music, founded in 1776 and patronized by royalty from 1785 onward. The Prince's wide knowledge of music was reflected in the programmes selected by him, which included works ranging from compositions by Henry VIII and Palestrina to Mozart and Cherubini. He was also a director of the Philharmonic Society. Music selected by him for concerts from 1843 to 1860 included the first performances in England of Schubert's Overture to *Fierabras*, of Schumann's Symphony in B Flat and of his cantata, *Das Paradies und die Peri*, with Jenny Lind as principal soloist.

Prince Albert's own compositions, several of which were published during his lifetime, included songs, chorales, a choral service and an anthem for the church. A chorale composed by the Prince was sung at the wedding of the Prince of Wales and Princess Alexandra in March 1863. His collection of music, another expression of the breadth of his taste, included early editions of Pergolesi and Haydn, contemporary publications and English opera libretti. Music meant everything to him, and he was anxious to see it taught universally in all schools.

The great change in Prince Albert's fortunes came with the advent of Sir Robert Peel as Prime Minister in August 1841. Aristocratic by education but rooted firmly in his middle-class origins, Peel, with his own love of the arts, was quick to realize the very valuable contribution Prince Albert could make to the cultural interests of his day. In September he invited the Prince to become chairman of a Royal Commission to consider the Promotion of the Fine Arts in connection with the rebuilding of the Houses of Parliament, which had been burnt down in 1834. It was a wonderful opportunity for the Prince to apply his knowledge of art, and, at the same time, demonstrate his ability as an administrator. Prince Albert insisted that members of the commission should be selected regardless of their party affiliations. He also suggested that discussion would be freer if no professional artist served on the commission, and although Charles Eastlake, later President of the Royal Academy and Director of the National Gallery, was appointed secretary, he was included in his capacity as an administrator. The Prince accepted the view already put forward that an experiment should be made in fresco technique. The idea was fostered by the fresco paintings of the Nazarenes, a derisory epithet given to an early nineteenth-century group of rebel German artists led by Franz Pforr and Johann Friedrich Overbeck, and later joined by Peter von Cornelius, who established themselves in Rome hoping to revitalize German art by emulating the simplicity and spiritual values of the pre-Renaissance masters. Cornelius soon returned to Germany however. His presence in London in 1841, and availability for consultation on the proposed decorative scheme for the Houses of Parliament, gave rise to rumours, promptly denied by Prince Albert, that foreign artists were to be employed. A competition was held and the artists, who included Daniel Maclise, William Dyce and C. W. Cope, were finally chosen. The whole decorative scheme was, however, not approved by Parliament until 1847, and money was not forthcoming until 1850. The project was not completed until after the Prince Consort's death.

In the meantime Prince Albert decided to try out for himself 'whether painting in fresco could be transplanted and made to flourish on English soil'. During 1843 the decoration of a small garden pavilion erected in the grounds of Buckingham Palace was carried out by several English painters, including Charles Eastlake, Edwin Landseer and Sir William Ross. Its central, octagonal room was furbished with eight lunettes, representing scenes from Milton's *Comus*, whilst the two side rooms were decorated, one with scenes from Sir Walter Scott's novels and poems, the other with Pompeian arabesques. A lithographed picture book of the decorations was published in 1846, with an introduction by the authoress, Mrs. Anna Jameson. The pavilion survived until 1928.

Prince Albert was not only a connoisseur of art, but also a skilled exponent. He learnt to paint in oil and watercolour and tried his hand at etching and lithography. Both he and the Queen took a personal interest in the Sketching Society founded by the fashionable portrait painter in watercolour, Alfred Edward Chalon, with his brother, John James Chalon, and Francis Stevens, going so far as to suggest subjects for study at two of the evening meetings in 1842.

Above all, the Prince was an ardent collector, being ahead of his time in acquiring paintings by the Primitive artists of north Italy, Germany and the Netherlands. For these he relied chiefly on the advice of Ludwig Grüner whom he had met in Rome, and who later purchased sculptures for the terraces at Osborne. Prince Albert's enthusiasm doubtless stemmed from his visit to Italy in 1839, when, writing to Prince Wilhelm von Löwenstein from Florence, he exclaimed, 'Oh, Florence, where I have been for two months, has gathered to herself noble treasures of art. I am often quite intoxicated with delight when I come out of one of the galleries.'

In 1848 a collection of paintings of early northern and Italian Schools, owned by an impecunious relative, Prince Ludwig von Oettingen-Wallerstein, and very much in line with Prince Albert's taste, came up for sale. Prince Ludwig had already sold the most valuable of his paintings by early German artists to Ludwig I, King of Bavaria, who added them to the Boisserée collection in the Alte Pinakothek, Munich. A catalogue was prepared and the pictures were exhibited at Kensington Palace in the hope that they might be acquired for the nation. In the end, however, Prince Albert, who had already acted as co-signatory of a promissory note for which the paintings were security, was obliged to purchase the collection himself. After his death, and in accordance with his wishes, a selection of the pictures was presented by Queen Victoria to the National Gallery in 1863.

Prince Albert made numerous purchases in other fields, including paintings by contemporary British artists. Among his watercolours were works by William Callow, at one time drawing master to the duc de Nemours and to his sister, Princess Clémentine d'Orléans, and who in 1863 was commissioned by Queen Victoria to make sketches of Rosenau; by David Roberts, one of the commissioners for the 1851 Exhibition; and by Joseph Nash. Paintings possibly commissioned by the Prince included *Eve of the Deluge* by the Romantic visionary John Martin and Charles West Cope's *Cardinal Wolsey Dying at the Gate of Leicester Abbey*. Though Turner exhibited a painting of *Schloss Rosenau* in 1841, he did not meet with royal favour.

Prince Albert's father died in January 1844. In February the Prince in an outburst of emotion wrote to Stockmar, 'A new epoch has commenced in my life ... my youth with all the recollections linked with it, has been buried with him around whom they centred. From that world I am forcibly torn away, and my whole thoughts diverted to my life and my own separate family.' Armed with this resolve, he was more than ever determined that he and the Queen should have some residence which would belong to them 'and not to the inquisitive and often impudent people'. Except at Claremont, which was King Leopold's property, Prince Albert and the Queen had no means of enjoying any privacy. As a seaside home the Pavilion at Brighton was both exotic and hemmed-in, so when Osborne House on the Isle of Wight, the property of Lady Isabella Blachford, came up for sale, they lost no time in negotiating for its purchase. It was the Prince's first real opportunity for indulging unrestrainedly his passion for gardening and estate management. From the start Osborne was to be Prince Albert's own creation. Independent of governmental interference, he selected as his partner in constructing the new Osborne the fashionable speculative builder, Thomas Cubitt, who was not only cooperative, but also willing to work to a fixed price contract. Cubitt needed no introduction as Anson was already living in one of Cubitt's houses in Eaton Place. In designing his Italianate mansion the Prince may well have been influenced by Cubitt's Albert Gate houses. For the interior decoration and garden lay-out he sought the advice of Ludwig Grüner. The Queen had been particularly impressed by the comfort of Sir Robert Peel's new house when she visited Drayton Manor in 1843, and no effort was spared in employing all the latest building techniques to render the new Osborne a thoroughly up-to-date and as near fireproof residence as possible. The gardens and the house were to blend in a harmonious unity, the brilliance of the flower-beds outdoors merging with the decorative colours within. Here indeed Prince Albert could revel 'in the enjoyment of the most glorious air, the most fragrant odours, the merriest choirs of birds, and the most luxuriant verdure'. For the Queen 'the deep blue sea ... the quiet and retirement', made Osborne 'a perfect paradise'.

Prior to her marriage the Queen had never travelled abroad. Relations with France were extremely strained in 1840 over Egypt, but recovered thanks largely to the Anglophile feelings of King Louis Philippe and the close links between the families of Coburg and Orléans which grew up after King Leopold's marriage to Louise d'Orléans.

In September 1843 the Queen and Prince Albert, on their new steam yacht *Victoria and Albert*, visited Louis Philippe at his country home at Eu in Normandy, it being thought not politic to visit Paris. Their reception by the Orléans family and the French population was extremely warm, and in the following year the King of the French returned their visit at Windsor.

In August 1845 the Queen made her first journey to Germany. Crossing Belgium, she was met at the Prussian frontier at Aachen by King Frederick William IV, who had come to England three years earlier to be godfather to the Prince of Wales. He entertained her at Schloss Brühl near Bonn and then at Schloss Stolzenfels, which he had restored, near Coblenz. Here she first met Princess Augusta, wife of the heir to the Prussian throne, who was to become one of her closest friends. The Queen was, however, very hurt that Prussian protocol gave precedence to an Austrian archduke over her husband, in contrast to French practice, and this always rankled with her. She sailed up the Rhine to Mainz, where the couple renewed acquaintance with Frau Siebold, and then drove by coach to Coburg where Prince Albert was able to show Queen Victoria his family home, which enchanted her with its Biedermeier patriarchalism.

The Golden Years 53

Prince Albert with the Princess Royal
Painting by Sir Edwin Landseer (Royal Collection)

Writing to his step-mother, Duchess Marie of Saxe-Coburg, in February 1843, Prince Albert observed, 'There is certainly a great charm, as well as deep interest in watching the development of feelings and faculties in a little child.' The Princess Royal was always his favourite child and perhaps of all his family best understood and appreciated the Prince's intellectual and political ideals. She was very precocious, and already by December 1843, when she was three years old, Prince Albert was writing to Baron Stockmar that 'Pussy' could now speak English and French 'with great fluency and choice of phrase'. The painting was a gift from the Prince to the Queen, 26 August 1842.

(*below*)
Windsor Castle in Modern Times: the Queen, Prince Albert and the Princess Royal at Windsor
Painting by Sir Edwin Landseer (Royal Collection)

Commissioned by the Queen in 1841, *Windsor Castle in Modern Times* was intended as a birthday gift for Prince Albert on 26 August. However, Landseer did not find it easy to complete, and the picture was not finished until 1843. The Queen's admiration for Landseer stemmed from her youth and was reciprocated by the artist, who considered the intellect of Queen Victoria superior to that of any woman in Europe. Landseer was offered a knighthood in 1842 but did not accept the honour until 1850. This felicitous domestic scene reflects the growing influence of the Prince, who, home from the shoot, fondles his pet greyhound, Eos, whilst the Queen looks on demurely. Eos, described by Prince Albert as a 'singularly clever creature', had been his companion from his fourteenth year and was cherished by him as a reminder of his youth. Eos died suddenly on 31 July 1844, and a bronze effigy was later placed on her grave in the park at Windsor.

54 The Golden Years

(*right*)
Victoria, Princess Royal (1840–1901)
Miniature by Guglielmo Faija after a painting by John Lucas (Royal Collection)

Faija later made his reputation as a portraitist by a tableau with eight miniatures of the English Royal Family, executed c. 1850. Vicky, who was 'such an amusement' to both the Queen and Prince Albert, is seen holding a miniature of her father by Sir William Ross.

(*below*)
H.M. The Queen with the Princess Royal and the Prince of Wales
Engraving by Samuel Cousins after a painting by Sir Edwin Landseer, 1843 (British Museum)

The Golden Years 55

56 The Golden Years

(*opposite top*)
The Royal Railroad Carriage, 1843
Coloured lithograph (British Museum)

(*opposite bottom*)
The Royal Family in Windsor Park, 1846
Coloured lithograph (British Museum)

(*right*)
Queen Victoria and Prince Albert Dancing
Titlepage to the *Cellarius Waltz*, coloured lithograph, c. 1840 (British Museum)

The Wonder of Windsor:
'The Artist, Poet, Fiddler, here we see,
And all is Tweedle-dum, and Tweedle-dee.'
Satirical lithograph by Charles Hunt, 1841 (British Museum)

From left to right: Prince Albert, seated at a desk; Ferdinand, King of Portugal, facing the window; playing the violin, Leopold, King of the Belgians; at the piano, Prince Ernest of Saxe-Coburg; the Queen; and in the doorway, the Duchess of Kent.

The Golden Years 57

58 *The Golden Years*

(*opposite*)
H.M. Queen Victoria and H.R.H. Prince Albert
Drawn from life from the Royal Box at the Italian Opera and published by John Field, 10 February 1841 (British Museum)

Both the Queen and Prince Albert inherited a love of music from their ancestors and went frequently to the opera. On their first visit to England in 1836 Albert and Ernest were taken to see Bellini's *I Puritani*, and were 'in perfect ecstasies, having never heard any of the singers before'. Princess Victoria's singing-master in 1836–37 was Luigi Lablache, one of the greatest basses of the nineteenth century, outstanding not only as a singer but as an actor as well. Lablache made his début at La Scala, Milan in 1817, but did not come to England until 1830 when he appeared in Cimarosa's *Il Matrimonio Segreto*.

The Queen found great enjoyment in Italian opera, but Prince Albert, more serious-minded, sought to introduce her to music of what he thought was a less frivolous nature. In a letter to the Princess Royal written in July 1860 he mentioned Gluck's *Orfeo* which he had seen twice and admired extremely. 'It is a real refreshment after our modern sound and fury, and the works of the Italian School.'

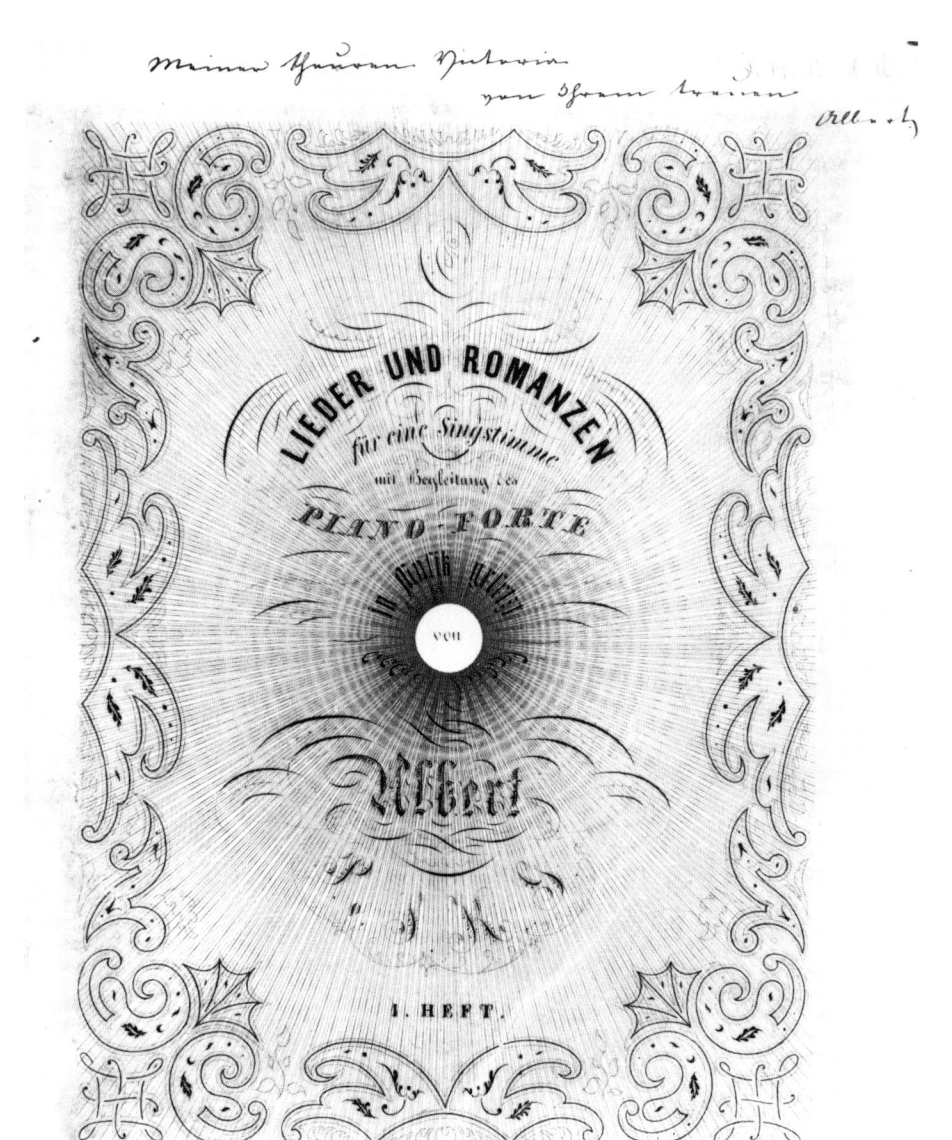

'Meiner theuren Victoria von Ihrem treuen Albert' ('To my dear Victoria from her faithful Albert')
Part two of *Lieder und Romanzen für eine Singstimme* mit Begleitung des Piano-Forte in Musik gesetzt von Albert P.v.S.K.G. [Prinz von Sachsen Koburg Gotha] 5 pt, Coburg 1838? (British Library)

The first three parts of the *Lieder* bear the Prince's autograph inscription and were presented by him to Queen Victoria before their marriage.

The Golden Years 59

'Farewell to Home'
Poetry by Prince Ernest. Written for his Brother. Music by Prince Albert (British Library)

This page comes from Prince Albert's own copy of *Songs and Ballads*, 'Written and set to music by their Royal Highnesses Albert and Ernest, Princes of Saxe Coburg and Gotha', published in London in 1840.

60 *The Golden Years*

Felix Mendelssohn (1809–1847)
Lithograph by G. Feckert after the painting by Eduard Magnus, 1844 (British Museum)

Shortly after Mendelssohn died, Queen Victoria wrote in her journal, 'To feel, when one is playing his beautiful music, that he is no more, seems incomprehensible.'

Felix Mendelssohn made his first public appearance in England in 1829. He conducted performances of his C Minor Symphony and his Overture to *A Midsummer Night's Dream* and was universally acclaimed. He afterwards visited Scotland, the inspiration of his *Hebrides Overture*. Mendelssohn paid several visits to England and was warmly received by both Queen Victoria and Prince Albert, who were well acquainted with and greatly admired his music. In August 1846 his oratorio, *Elijah*, was given at the Birmingham Music Festival and was a tremendous success. He returned in 1847 to conduct further performances of a revised version, evoking the praise of Prince Albert. Immediately after a performance attended by him and the Queen on 23 April, Prince Albert sent his copy of the libretto to the composer with the inscription, 'To the Noble Artist who ... has been able, by his genius and science, like another Elijah, faithfully to preserve the worship of true art.'

Mendelssohn first met Jenny Lind in 1844. The attraction was mutual, and from then on they performed together at concerts whenever possible. The painting after which this lithograph was made, was presented by Magnus to Jenny Lind.

Jenny Lind (1820–1887)
Replica of the painting by Eduard Magnus, 1846 (National Portrait Gallery)

Writing to the manager of the Birmingham Music Festival in 1846, Mendelssohn said of Jenny Lind, 'I consider her without hesitation as the absolutely first singer of the day and perhaps of many days to come.' Queen Victoria and Prince Albert first heard 'the Swedish Nightingale' at an evening concert, conducted by Giacomo Meyerbeer, during their visit to the King and Queen of Prussia at Brühl in 1845 on their way to Coburg.

Owing to certain contract difficulties, Jenny Lind did not appear in London until 4 May 1847, when her performance as Alice in Meyerbeer's *Robert le Diable* was a resounding success. The Royal Family turned out in force. Queen Victoria, Prince Albert, Queen Adelaide and the Duchess of Kent were in the royal box, whilst the Duke and Duchess of Cambridge, ministers and ambassadors swelled the audience. Also present were Mendelssohn and that 'good old soul' Lablache. At the final curtain, the Queen, in unwitting imitation of the Empress of Austria, who on a previous occasion had cast her wreath on to the stage, now threw her own bouquet at Jenny's feet in ecstatic appreciation. But in spite of all her triumphs Jenny Lind left the stage in 1849 and devoted herself henceforth to concert singing, especially of oratorios, giving many performances for charity.

In 1852 Jenny Lind was married in Boston, Massachusetts, to the pianist and composer, Otto Goldschmidt. Her last appearance in England was at a charity concert at Malvern in 1883. She died in 1887. A plaque to her memory was unveiled in Westminster Abbey by Princess Christian (Queen Victoria's third daughter, Helena) on 20 April 1894.

Four Etchings by Prince Albert (British Museum)

Etching was a favourite pastime of the Queen and Prince Albert during the first four years of their marriage. It provided the Queen with an interest when she was precluded from public life in the weeks preceding the birth of her children. Her first plate, dated 28 August 1840, was made under the guidance of Sir George Hayter. From 1842 onward she had lessons from Sir Edwin Landseer, Prince Albert giving her advice and correcting her proofs. Sometimes they worked together on one plate. The Queen's etchings were at first very simple, portrayals of her pet dogs and of the children. Prince Albert was more venturesome, and he made more use of hatching. He executed etchings of imaginary scenes from literature. from drawings by the Queen and after pictures in the Royal Collection, also of the children and pet dogs. There is no evidence that either the Queen or the Prince printed their own plates.

Two Heads of Eagles, 1841
After the drawing in reverse, by Agostino Carracci in the Royal Collection

Wallenstein and his Servant, 1840
A scene from Schiller's drama *Wallenstein*

62 *The Golden Years*

The Princess Royal and the Prince of Wales, 1843
After a sketch by Queen Victoria

Eos and Cairnach, 1844
After a sketch in reverse, drawn from recollection by Edwin Landseer, in the Royal Collection

Eos, the Prince's beloved greyhound, died on 31 July 1844. Cairnach was a favourite Skye terrier of Queen Victoria.

The Golden Years 63

The Coronation of the Virgin
Triptych by Giusto de' Menabuoi (National Gallery)

This painting by Menabuoi, a Florentine active in Padua (1363/64–1387/91) and often known as Giusto Padovano, originally formed part of the collection of Prince Ludwig von Oettingen-Wallerstein's early Italian paintings, purchased by Prince Albert in 1848. It was presented by the Queen to the National Gallery in 1863.

64 *The Golden Years*

Franz Xaver Winterhalter (1806–1873)
Woodcut (British Museum)

Winterhalter made a reputation for himself in Karlsruhe, where his portraits of Leopold, Grand Duke of Baden and of Grand Duchess Sophia led to his appointment as court painter. In 1834 he went to Paris, achieving success there with his portraits of Queen Marie Amélie, King Louis Philippe and other members of the Orléans family. His work was commissioned by most of the reigning families in Europe, his sitters including Leopold I of Belgium, Napoleon III and the Empress Eugénie, the Emperor Francis Joseph of Austria and the Prince and Princess of Prussia.

In 1841 Queen Victoria summoned him to London, and from 1842 on a constant stream of portraits of the Queen, Prince Albert and other members of the Royal Family were produced by Winterhalter. Formal in manner, he created a flattering image of the Royal Family, emphasizing in his groupings of the Queen and her children the splendour and exaltation made possible, as Prince Albert expressed it, 'only through the personal character of the Sovereign'.

His output was prolific and to aid him in executing the vast number of replicas requested for exchange among his illustrious patrons, Winterhalter enlisted the assistance of his brother, Hermann, whose style bore an uncanny resemblance to his own. Winterhalter died in 1873, the same year as Landseer. Queen Victoria wrote to the Empress Augusta, 'Winterhalter's death is a terrible grief to me, he is an irreparable loss! . . . So many memories go to the grave with him!'

(*below*)
Florinda
Painting by Franz Xaver Winterhalter (Royal Collection)

Illustrating an episode in Robert Southey's *Roderick, the Last of the Goths*, this painting was a birthday gift from Queen Victoria to Prince Albert in 1852 and hung in the Pavilion at Osborne. In style and composition, *Florinda* anticipates Winterhalter's *Empress Eugénie and her Ladies*, so greatly admired by the Queen on her visit to Paris in 1855, a watercolour of which was subsequently given by her to Prince Albert. Queen Victoria made the observation in 1860 that the head of one of the figures in *Florinda* resembled that of the Princess Carolyne zu Sayn-Wittgenstein, the companion of Liszt.

The Golden Years 65

(*below*)
Osborne House, October 1844
Watercolour by C. R. Stanley (Royal Collection)

By 1843 it was apparent to the Queen and Prince Albert that if they were to enjoy any privacy in their home life they would have to find a house well away from their official residences. When Sir Robert Peel suggested that Lady Isabella Blachford might be willing to sell Osborne House, on the Isle of Wight, Prince Albert lost no time in investigating the site. He visited it in March 1844, and the Queen stayed in the 'very comfortable little house' in the following October. From the outset Thomas Cubitt, the builder, warned the Prince that the construction of a new house would be inevitable. Though the new building resulted in a grandiose Italianate mansion, Prince Albert wrote to his step-mother in 1847, 'When we are in the Isle of Wight, where we are not surrounded by a court and its formalities, our life is so quiet and simple.'

(*bottom*)
Osborne under Construction, March 1847
Watercolour by W. L. Leitch (Royal Collection)

The foundation stone for the new house at Osborne was laid by Queen Victoria on 23 June 1845. By September 1846 the Pavilion, containing the Queen's private apartments, was ready for occupation. Work on the household wing then began and continued through 1847, during which time a start was made on demolishing the old house. Not only the new mansion itself, but also the elaborately designed terraces, descending toward the lawn and sea, largely the work of Prince Albert, were developed stage by stage. These were expensive to construct, the upper terrace, shown in Leitch's watercolour, calling for a massive retaining wall. The terraces were not completed until 1854.

66 *The Golden Years*

Osborne, the Swiss Cottage, 1855
Watercolour by W. L. Leitch (Royal Collection)

In a letter to Queen Victoria, dated 7 July 1851, Princess Feodora wrote, 'I have had a little Swiss cottage built in the garden [at Schloss Langenburg], which belongs to the children and this morning it was opened by Feo and Ada [her daughters] as their own; it contains one room and a kitchen.'

During 1853–54 a genuine wooden chalet was brought in sections from Switzerland and erected in the grounds of Osborne, about half a mile to the east of the house. There, in a Rousseau-esque manner, the Queen's children found amusement and instruction. The young Princes practised carpentry and gardening, whilst the Princesses learned cooking in a kitchen equipped with the most up-to-date fittings. In addition to a dining-room and a dressing-room, the chalet contained a sitting-room where the children could entertain their parents and friends.

The Golden Years 67

(opposite top)
The Great Exhibition in Hyde Park, 1851, from the Serpentine
Watercolour by William Wyld (Royal Collection) *see chapter five*

(opposite bottom)
Balmoral Castle, 1860
Watercolour by George Arthur Fripp (Royal Collection) *see chapter six*

Fripp was born in Bristol in 1813, moved to London in 1841 and became a full member of the Old Watercolour Society in 1845. In 1860 he was commissioned by Queen Victoria to execute a series of watercolour drawings of the scenery around Balmoral.

Staying at Balmoral in September 1863, nearly two years after the Prince Consort's death, Queen Victoria wrote to Queen Augusta of Prussia, 'In this house I see him, hear him, search for him everywhere! I go more out of doors... The wild, grim, solitary mountains, where no human soul is, comfort me! The mountains, the woods, the rocks seem to talk of him, for he wandered and climbed so often among them.'

Meeting of the Fine Arts Commissioners, 1846
Preparatory sketch by John Partridge for his larger picture of the Royal Fine Arts Commission (National Portrait Gallery)

The Prince is seated below the bust of Queen Victoria. On his right are Charles Eastlake, Secretary of the Commission, Sir Robert Peel and Lord John Russell; on his left, Lord Melbourne, Viscount Palmerston, the Earl of Aberdeen; and standing before a model of the building, the architect, Charles Barry.

The Fine Arts Commission was appointed in 1841 to consider plans in connection with the decoration of the new Houses of Parliament. The old Houses of Parliament were destroyed by fire in 1834, and in 1835 a competition was announced for designs for a new building, 'the style to be Gothic or Elizabethan'. In February 1836, Barry, who had already achieved a reputation for his versatility and skill, notably through his designs for the Royal Institution of Fine Arts in Manchester, the Travellers' Club in Pall Mall and King Edward VI's School in Birmingham, won the award. He knew Eastlake, and was well acquainted with the architect, Augustus Welby Pugin, a passionate advocate of Neo-Gothic, who worked on the detailed drawings. Progress on the building was slow, and Barry, who was knighted in 1852 when the Houses of Lords and Commons were nearing completion, died in 1860. The finalization of his work was entrusted to his son, Edward Middleton Barry.

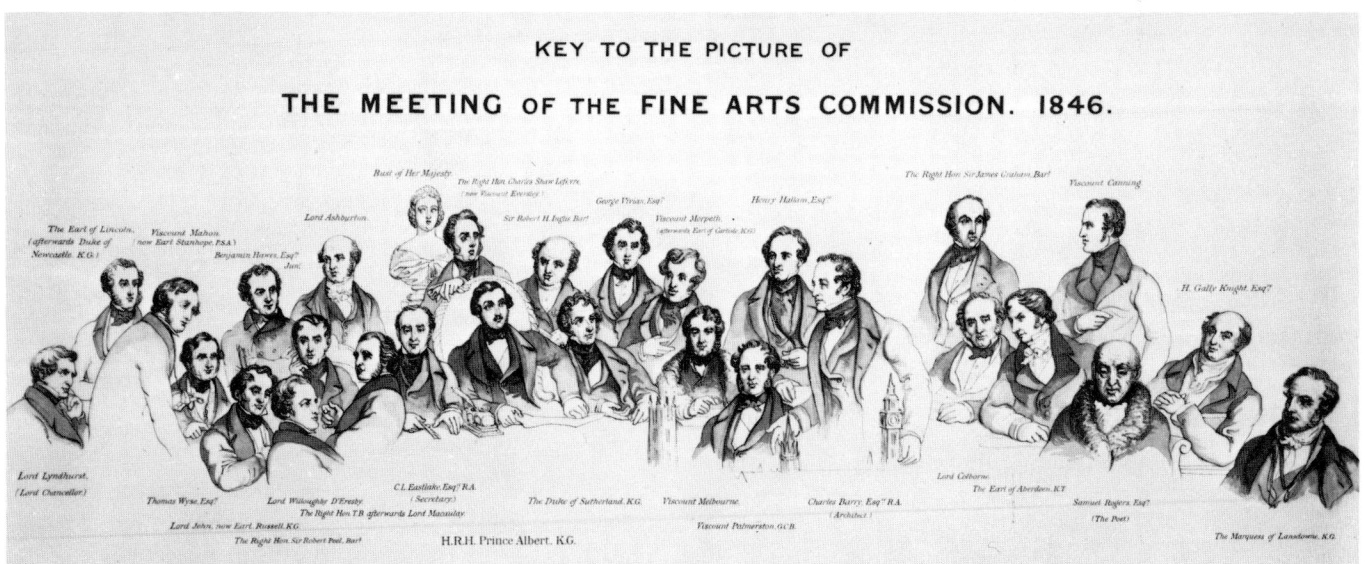

68 *The Golden Years*

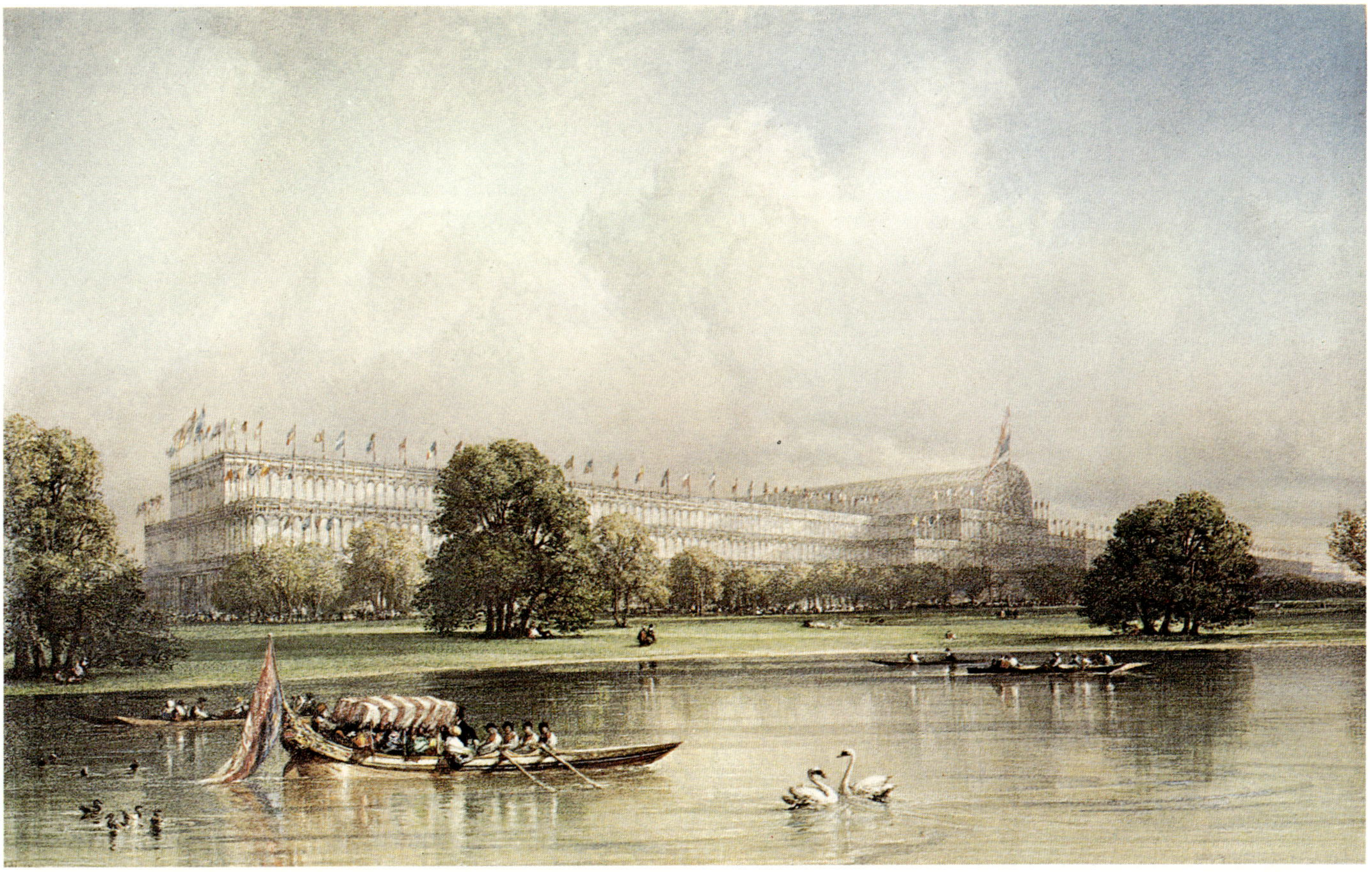

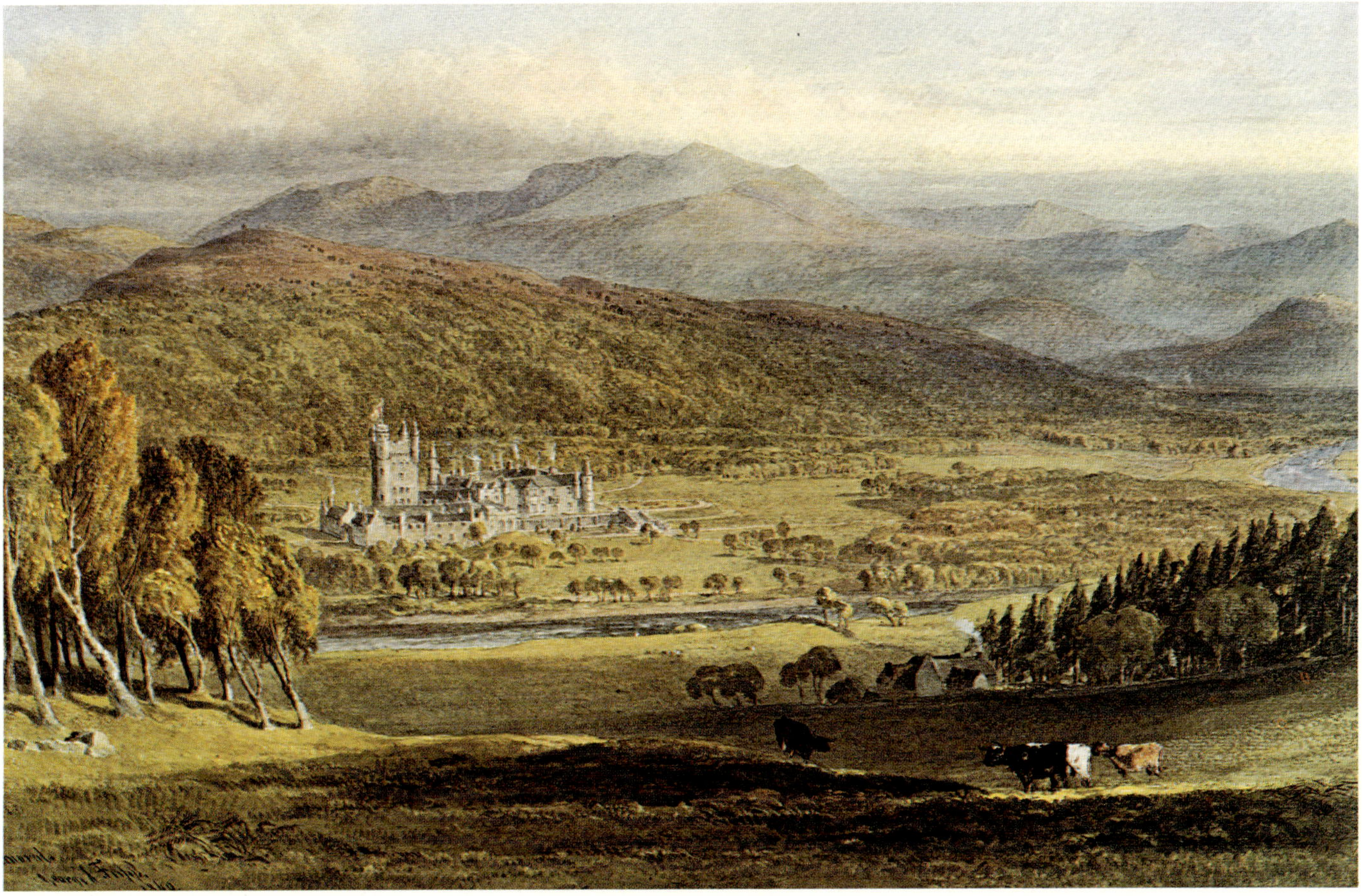

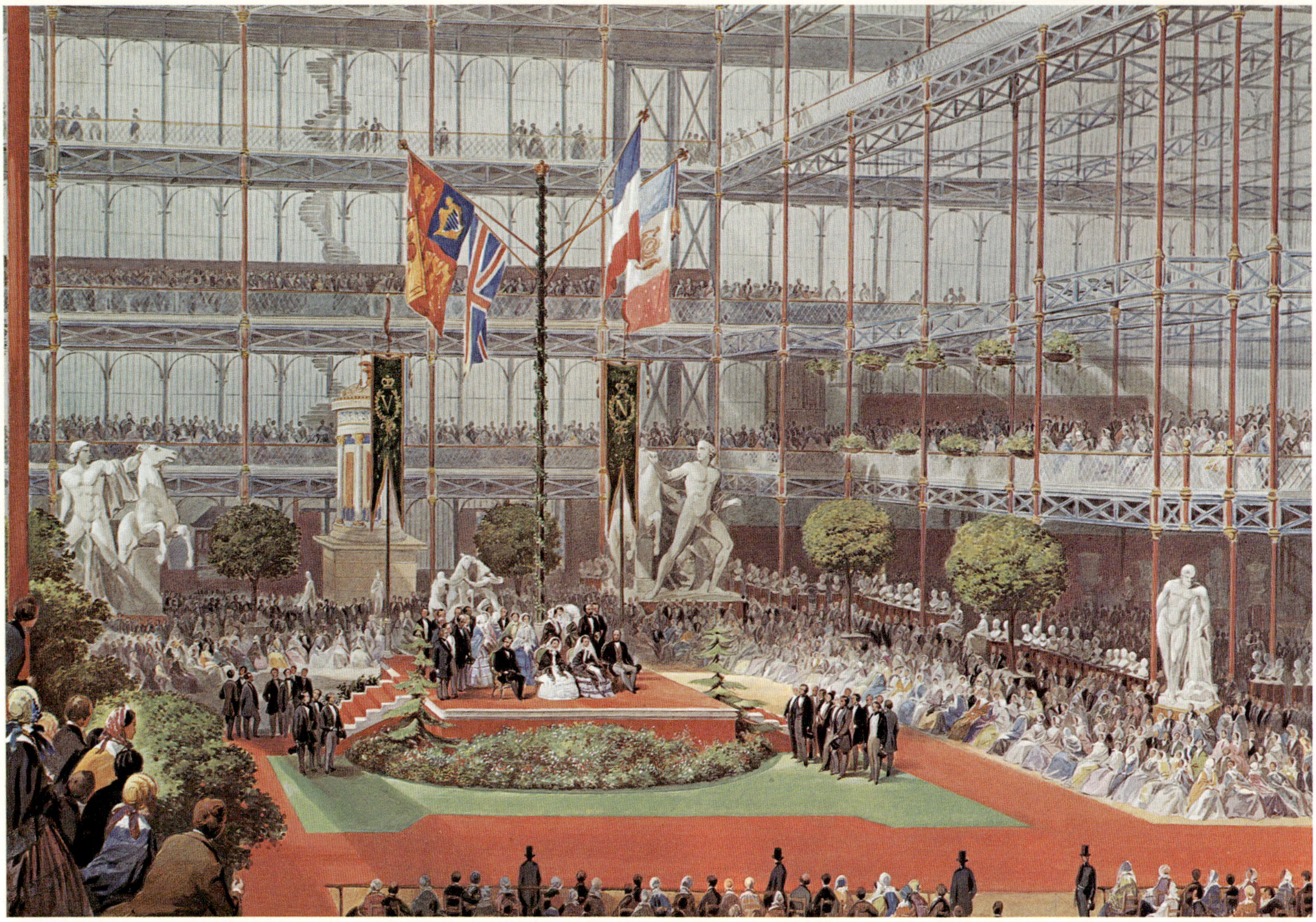

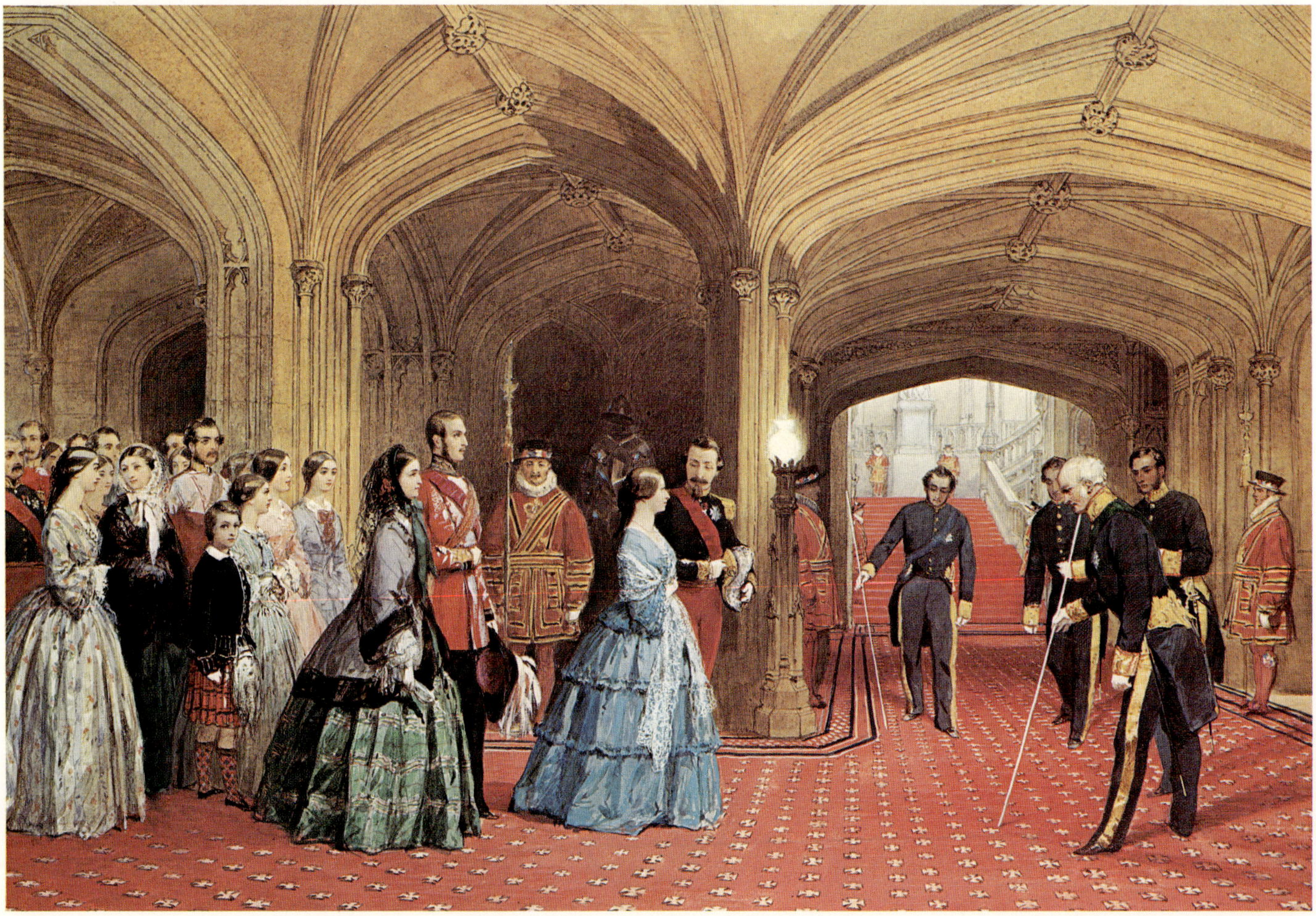

(*opposite top*)
The Imperial and Royal Visit to the Crystal Palace, 20 April 1855
Watercolour by J. Roberts after Louis Haghe (Royal Collection) *see chapter six*

This visit took place on the Emperor's birthday, and he was affected by the private congratulations and gifts of the Royal Family. The party drove to the Crystal Palace, recently re-erected at Sydenham.

(*opposite bottom*)
The Reception of the Emperor and Empress of the French at Windsor Castle, 16 April 1855
Watercolour by G. H. Thomas (Royal Collection) *see chapter six*

Prince Albert met the Emperor and Empress at Dover and escorted them across an enthusiastic London to Windsor, where the Queen waited with her children. The band struck up *Partant pour la Syrie*, the song with words by the Emperor's mother, Queen Hortense, and music by M. Labord, which was adopted as the national hymn of the Second Empire.

'I cannot say what indescribable emotions filled me, how much it felt like a wonderful dream,' wrote the Queen. 'I advanced and embraced the Emperor, who received two salutes, on either cheek from me, having first kissed my hand. I next embraced the very gentle, graceful and evidently very nervous Empress. We presented each the Princes and our children (Vicky and Bertie) and then we went up the Grand Stairs, Albert leading the Empress, who in the most graceful manner refused to go first, but at length, with graceful reluctance did so... We went into the Throne Room, where we presented the five other children to whom they were very kind... The Emperor was in uniform. He is extremely short, but with a head and bust which ought to belong to a much taller man. She is taller; was in a plain plaid silk dress and straw bonnet, with a black velvet mantilla. She is most grateful and pleasing, with a very charming kind expression.' Such was Queen Victoria's own description of this historic scene. The harmony and happiness of that initial moment were to continue throughout the visit and form the basis of a lifelong friendship.

The building was empty when they arrived, and they were able to walk quietly through the nave and all the courts, the Alhambra particularly pleasing the Empress. 'The crowds assembled below were quite enormous, and the cheering very enthusiastic for each of us, my beloved Albert being asked for and warmly received. The dear Empress always puts herself in the background,' recorded Queen Victoria.

After a private lunch they walked again through the transept, now crowded with 30,000–40,000 people, on to the balcony to see the fountains play and then on to an estrade in front of banners bearing the letters 'N' and 'V'. 'Nothing could have succeeded better,' wrote the Queen, 'I felt as I walked at the Emperor's arm, that I was possibly a protection for him.' The Emperor was enchanted with the Crystal Palace and commented, 'It is superb! What a place for a fête!'

The Arrival of Queen Victoria at Granton, 1842
Watercolour by William Joy (Royal Collection)

When Queen Victoria, with Prince Albert, visited Scotland in 1842 she was the first English monarch, with the exception of George IV who went to Holyrood in 1822, to set foot on Scottish soil since Charles I. Due to Chartist riots in the Midlands and north of England, they journeyed by sea, embarking at Woolwich on 29 August on the sailing yacht *Royal George*, commanded by Lord Adolphus Fitzclarence, a natural son of William IV and Mrs. Jordan. Lord Adolphus reported to Charles Greville that 'nothing could be more agreeable and amiable than she was (and the Prince too) on board the yacht, conversing all the time with perfect ease and good humour... dining on deck in the midst of the Sailors, making them dance, talking to the boatswain.'

Due to bad weather on the second evening, they were late in arriving and only anchored off Inchkeith, near Edinburgh, at 1 a.m. on 1 September. Soon after breakfast they landed at Granton Pier, where the Duke of Buccleuch and Sir Robert Peel were waiting to receive them. They returned home in the *Trident*, a steam vessel, whose performance so impressed the Queen that she ordered the building of a new royal steam yacht, the *Victoria and Albert*, which was launched on 25 April 1843, the day on which Princess Alice was born.

The Golden Years 71

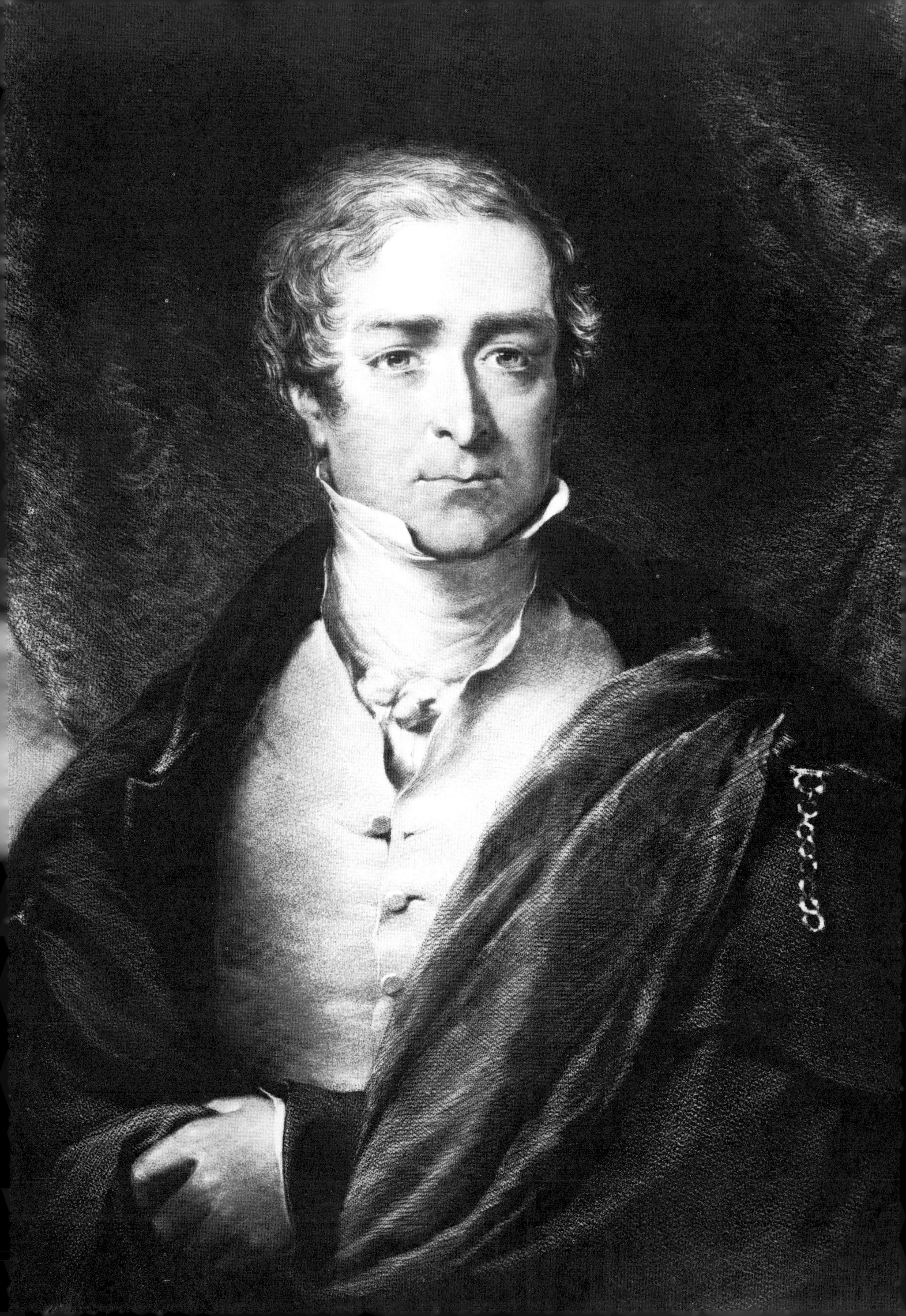

Sir Robert Peel, Bt. (1788–1850)
Engraving after a painting by John Deffett Francis, 1842 (British Museum)

King Leopold wrote to Queen Victoria after the death of Sir Robert Peel, 'You and Albert lose in him a friend whose moderation, correct judgment, great knowledge of everything connected with the country, can never be found again.' Prince Albert echoed this in a speech at York in October, 'The constitution of Sir Robert Peel's mind was peculiarly that of a statesman, and of an English statesman: he was liberal from feeling but conservative upon principle.'

Peel first entered Parliament as a Tory in 1809. As Home Secretary under Wellington he instituted the Metropolitan Police, popularly known as 'Bobbies'. Opposed to both Catholic emancipation and parliamentary reform, he accepted them once enacted, and in his 'Tamworth Manifesto' of 1834 set the course of the Conservative Party as one of genuine reform. After reintroducing Pitt's income tax as a basis of sound finance, Peel moved towards Free Trade and the abolition of the Corn Laws in 1846, when he was able to carry his Cabinet virtually entirely, but not the backbenchers.

Prince Albert found in Peel a mentor, whose sympathies and cultural activities were very akin to his own. Both were keenly interested in art and science, collecting paintings and experimenting with new methods of farming. Both recognized the need for social reform, Peel realizing only too well the resentments which were fermenting 'under the glowing surface of our modern civilisation'. He was no believer in the distribution of honours, refusing the Garter for himself in 1842. He shared Prince Albert's love of the country. Returning from a visit to Scotland in October 1849, Peel wrote to Lord Aberdeen, 'It would be painful for me to think, what is very probable, that I shall never see the Highlands again,' a curious premonition, perhaps, of his death on 2 July 1850.

Blair, looking towards Killiecrankie: Departure of the Duchess of Kent, 5 August 1850
Watercolour by William Evans (Royal Collection)

Blair Atholl is only about three miles distant from the Pass of Killiecrankie, where in 1689 the Highlanders routed William III's army, although in the hour of victory their commander, 'Bonny Dundee', was mortally wounded and carried to Blair Atholl to die. In September 1844 Queen Victoria and Prince Albert, accompanied by their eldest child, the Princess Royal, paid a second visit to Scotland. They stayed at Blair Castle, lent to them by Lord and Lady Glenlyon. Their sojourn at Blair, where Prince Albert was in ecstasies over the magnificent scenery and 'Pussy' was 'learning Gaelic, but making wild work with the names of the mountains', only confirmed for the Queen and the Prince the appeal of the Highlands, where 'there was a quiet, a retirement, a wildness, a liberty, and a solitude that had such a charm for us.'

The Duchess of Kent visited Scotland for the first time in 1850 and was present with the Queen at the Braemar Gathering. She subsequently stayed every summer at Abergeldie until ill-health prevented her from undertaking the long journey.

The Golden Years 73

Louis Philippe, King of the French (1773–1850)
Miniature by Sir William Ross (Royal Collection)

The eldest son of Philippe 'Egalité', duc d'Orléans, the future king was brought up by Madame de Genlis according to the tenets of Rousseau's *Emile*. He followed his father in supporting the French Revolution, but deserted from the republican army with Dumouriez to the headquarters of Prince Frederick Josias of Coburg, though declining a command under him.

Louis Philippe emigrated to the United States and then to Halifax, Nova Scotia, where, through Madame de Saint-Laurent, a former acquaintance, he met Prince Edward, Duke of Kent. In 1800 he settled in Twickenham with a pension from Pitt. There he renewed his friendship with the Duke of Kent and also became friendly with Princess Charlotte and Prince Leopold. His eventful life made him very flexible and an outward bonhomie often masked cunning and ambition.

Louis Philippe returned to France at the Restoration in 1814 and became a rallying point for the interests created by the Revolution of 1789. That of July 1830 deposed his Bourbon cousin, Charles X, and made Louis Philippe King of the French. The style of the Orléans monarchy was constitutional and the public image of the king that essentially of a conventional bourgeois; his sons, for instance, were educated at lycées.

After Queen Victoria visited him at Eu, Louis Philippe returned the visit at Windsor in 1844 to the delight of the English Queen, who wrote to King Leopold, 'The King praised my dearest Albert most highly and fully appreciated his great qualities and talents; and what gratifies me *so much*, treats him completely as his equal, calling him "Mon Frère" and saying to me that *my husband* was the same as me, which it is—and "Le Prince Albert, c'est pour moi le Roi" ' (17 October 1844). On this occasion the French king was invested with the Order of the Garter which made him feel an equal among the sovereigns of Europe.

On his return to France Louis Philippe sent presents to the Prince of Wales and the Princess Royal, writing to the Queen, 'All I desire is that your children may one day recall having seen one who was the faithful friend of their grandfather, as he is and will always be of their beloved parents' (15 November 1844). After the 1848 revolution the King fled with his wife and family to England and resided at Claremont, the property of his son-in-law King Leopold, where he died.

Marie Amélie, Queen of the French (1782–1866)
Miniature by Frédéric Millet (Royal Collection)

The daughter of Ferdinand IV, King of Naples and Queen Maria Carolina, a sister of Marie Antoinette and the friend of Nelson and Lady Hamilton, Marie Amélie married the exiled duc d'Orléans at Palermo in 1809 under the protection of the British fleet. She and Louis Philippe had five sons and three daughters, who gave France a fine example of united family life under the July Monarchy.

Prince Albert wrote to Stockmar (10 September 1843), 'The family of Louis Philippe have a strong feeling that for the last thirteen years they have been placed under a ban, as though they were lepers, by all Europe, and by every Court, and expelled from the society of reigning Houses, and therefore they rate very highly the visit of the most powerful sovereign in Europe. The King said this to me over and over again.' This boycott helped to bring about four marriages between the Houses of Orléans and Coburg and made relations between them specially close.

Queen Marie Amélie told Victoria she had always had a maternal feeling for her and commended her children to the Queen and Prince Albert 'que vous les protégiez; ce sont des amis de coeur'. When Queen Victoria visited Napoleon III, she was at pains to explain to him that her friendship for him could not inhibit her warm feelings for the House of Orléans to whom she and Prince Albert were closely related.

74 The Golden Years

Medal
Issued to Commemorate the Reception of Queen Victoria by King Louis Philippe at Le Tréport, 2 September 1843 (British Museum)

The obverse depicts the King greeting the Queen, and her enthusiastic reception at Le Tréport, some two miles from Eu. The Queen and Prince Albert travelled on the *Victoria and Albert* and were met off Cherbourg by the sailor prince de Joinville, Louis Philippe's third son. The King came out in the royal barge with two more sons to meet the Queen, and the two royal standards of England and France flew side by side.

The Château d'Eu
Watercolour by Lady Canning (Royal Collection)

This château in Normandy is on the site of a fortress before whose walls Duke Rollo, Queen Victoria's remotest Norman ancestor, was killed. The building, begun by the duc de Guise in 1581, was completed in the following century by Louis XIV's cousin Mademoiselle de Montpensier. It was inherited in 1821 by Louis Philippe, then duc d'Orléans, on the death of his mother, heiress of the ducs de Penthièvre, who stemmed from the illegitimate issue of Louis XIV and Madame de Montespan. Louis Philippe enlarged and beautified the château considerably, and it became the country home of the Orléans family, to be expropriated with their other properties in 1852 by Napoleon III. It was here, from 2 to 7 September 1843, that the Queen and the Prince visited the King and Queen of the French and their family. 'I feel at home with them all, as if I were one of them,' Queen Victoria wrote in her journal.

The Golden Years 75

76 *The Golden Years*

(*opposite*)
The Leave-taking in Queen Victoria's Cabin on board the 'Victoria and Albert', 7 September 1843
Watercolour by Franz Xaver Winterhalter (Royal Collection)

'At last the mauvais moment arrived and we were obliged to take leave and with very great regret,' Queen Victoria wrote in her journal after this happy and successful visit *en famille*. Left to right are the King's sons, the ducs de Montpensier and d'Aumâle and the prince de Joinville with the princesse, sister of the Emperor of Brazil, and Queen Marie Amélie. Queen Victoria is shaking the hand of King Louis Philippe, while behind her stands Prince Albert. To the right of the King are Queen Louise of the Belgians; Madame Adélaïde, the King's sister; the recently widowed duchesse d'Orléans, wife of Louis Philippe's eldest son; Princess Clémentine, another daughter of the King and wife of Prince Augustus of Saxe-Coburg-Kohary; and Admiral Mackau. The prince de Joinville returned with the Queen and Prince Albert to Brighton for two days, 'It was a pleasure to keep Joinville, who is so amiable and our great favourite,' wrote the Queen.

Leopold I, King of the Belgians (1790–1865)
Miniature by Magdalen Ross (Royal Collection)

Linked by his marriage to the daughter of Louis Philippe, Leopold fostered the close relationship between the Houses of Coburg and Orléans, both regarded as pariahs by legitimists for assuming crowns to which they had no right, with further dynastic links with Portugal and Spain. Corresponding with the Queen and Prince Albert, Leopold was the focal point of the Coburg network throughout western Europe.

By 1848 his personal relations with Austria had improved and his earlier sympathies with German national unity had faded. After the Second Empire had replaced the Orléans monarchy, the King initiated a rapprochement with the Bonapartes by welcoming Prince Napoleon-Joseph to Brussels, thus setting off a process which culminated in Queen Victoria and Prince Albert's exchange of visits with Napoleon III. Like Prince Albert, however, King Leopold always entertained suspicions of the aims of the French Emperor, especially as to Bonapartist threats to Belgian independence.

Louise, Queen of the Belgians (1812–1850)
Miniature by Magdalen Ross after Sir William Ross (Royal Collection)

The eldest daughter of Louis Philippe, Louise was married in 1832 to Leopold I and thus became the ancestress of the Belgian Royal House. Called by her mother, whom she resembled, 'the angel of the family', Queen Louise sensed that her marriage was a political transaction and that her husband still mourned his first wife, Princess Charlotte, after whom their only daughter, the tragic Empress of Mexico, was named. Queen Louise became a close friend to her husband's niece, the then Princess Victoria, and hoped that the young Queen would marry her Orléans brother, the duc de Nemours. She was, therefore, somewhat disappointed, according to Ernest II of Saxe-Coburg, when Victoria chose Prince Albert. Magdalen Ross (Mrs. Edwin Dalton, 1801–74), the sister of Sir William Ross, was appointed Miniature Painter to the Queen in 1850.

Reception of King Louis Philippe at Windsor, 8 October 1844
Painting by Franz Xaver Winterhalter (Royal Collection)

In the centre of the Grand Reception Room stands the Queen, holding the Prince of Wales by the hand. Beside her are the Princess Royal and Princess Alice, while behind her are the Duchess of Kent and the nurse, Mrs. Perkins, carrying Prince Alfred. The row of gentlemen behind the ladies includes the Duke of Wellington, Sir Robert Peel and the Earl of Aberdeen.

King Louis Philippe advances towards the Queen, presented by Prince Albert and followed by his youngest son, the duc de Montpensier. The Queen was charmed with the latter and at her instigation 'Bertie [the Prince of Wales] has immediately taken a passion for Montpensier.' Montpensier's marriage two years later to the younger sister of Isabella II, Queen of Spain was to disrupt the Anglo-French *entente cordiale* of which this visit marked the apogee. On the right, his left hand in his vest, is François Guizot, the French Prime Minister, who, during enforced retirement after the 1848 revolution, published a life of Peel and a translation of Prince Albert's speeches.

The Golden Years 77

Christmas Trees at Windsor: the Royal Children and the Duchess of Kent's Trees, 1850
Watercolour by J. Roberts (Royal Collection)

Writing to his step-mother on 26 December 1847, Prince Albert remarked, 'I must now seek in the children an echo of what Ernest and I were in the old time, of what we felt and thought; and their delight in the Christmas-trees is not less than ours used to be.'

From early childhood both Queen Victoria and Prince Albert rejoiced in a Christmas eve 'entirely German and *gemütlich*', when gifts, laid out on individual tables, were exchanged in the radiant glow of candle-lit trees. After the present-giving the candles were extinguished, to be relit on Christmas Day, on New Year's Day and on Twelfth Night when gingerbread was an established feature of the decoration. Trees hung with sweetmeats, fruits and toys and illuminated with small wax candles were known at the Christmas parties of Queen Charlotte, consort of George III, of Queen Adelaide and of the Duchess of Kent. It was left, however, to Prince Albert and Queen Victoria to establish the tree as a popular symbol, the Queen making a special point of presenting trees to barracks and schools where children's parties were being held.

78 The Golden Years

Queen Victoria's Birthday Tables, 1861
Watercolour by J. Roberts (Royal Collection)

Gifts were laid out on tables for birthdays in the same manner as at Christmas. In a letter to Princess Augusta of Prussia, Prince Albert wrote in 1858, 'Although birthday congratulations are all much the same, and as one gets older one looks forward less eagerly to them, the need to express them is still a need of heart, and the receipt of them brings hearts closer together.'

The Golden Years 79

The First of May
Painting by Franz Xaver Winterhalter (Royal Collection)

This picture not only commemorates the opening of the Great Exhibition, visible in the background, but also the birthdays of Prince Arthur, later Duke of Connaught, aged one, and of his godfather, the Duke of Wellington, aged eighty-two. Queen Victoria records the Duke's visit to his godson in the afternoon of 1 May. 'He came to us both at five, and gave him a golden cup and some toys, which he had himself chosen, and Arthur gave him a nosegay.'

Winterhalter had apparently no idea how to execute such a painting, so, according to Queen Victoria, 'Dear Albert with his wonderful knowledge and taste' was called in to assist. As Michael Levey remarks, 'The composition is a sort of deliberately secularized *Adoration of the Magi,* giving a holy aura to the good domestic life of Queen and Prince.'

'Those two Dreadful Old Men' and the Great Exhibition

Prince Albert was fortunate that the first six years of his life in England, during which he found his feet, were dominated by the eclipse of Melbourne and the rule of Peel. He found no British statesman more congenial than Peel, who looked forward rather than back and had more understanding than most for Germany and its problems, so dear to Albert's heart.

The Prince, like Peel, regarded the abolition of the Corn Laws and the advent of Free Trade as an inevitable step in the progress of the modern industrial society. Sir Robert Peel was able to win the support of his Cabinet and ministers for his policy, but not that of the mass of Tory backbenchers, country squires nervous for their rent rolls from farmers. The Conservative Party, which he had rebuilt after the Reform Act of 1832, was riven in two. Greville aptly described the schism of 1846 as producing 'a final separation between the able few and the numerous mediocrity of the Party'. The Protectionists were a shepherdless flock rejecting the name 'Conservative' because it reminded them of Peel, until they found a leader of genius in Disraeli, while the Peelites looked vainly to a leader who was thankful to be released from averting the dangers threatening 'a set of men with great possessions and little foresight, who call themselves Conservatives and Protectionists, and whose only chance of safety is that their counsels shall not be followed'. Peel waited in the wings, but his death following a riding accident in 1850 was a tragic blow to the English parliamentary scene.

It left in unchallenged personal domination the Foreign Secretary Viscount Palmerston, whom the Whig Prime Minister, Lord John Russell, was quite unable to control. The combination of these two 'Dreadful Old Men' was anathema to the Queen, as to the Prince, and there were repeated clashes between court and Cabinet as Europe was swept by revolution in 1848/49 and Prince Albert saw the thrones of his relations crumbling.

The Prince believed in German unity under monarchic leadership and in the right of the Schleswig-Holsteiners to join it, while distrusting Italian unity as likely to make Italy dependent on the expansionist French Republic and to weaken Austria as a counterpoise to Russia. Palmerston, on the other hand, was suspicious of German unity and wished to maintain the integrity of the Danish monarchy. For Palmerston and Russell Italian unity, moreover, harmonized with their inbred Whig prejudices against Catholicism and absolutism. Fundamental divergences of view were compounded by differences concerning methods. Palmerston sought to determine British policy on his own, often leaving the Queen insufficient time for perusal and decision. When Lord John wrote to the Prince (19 June 1849) on Palmerston's authority that during 1848 no less than 28,000 despatches were handled by the Foreign Office, the Prince replied that 'these 28,000 despatches in the year, Lord Palmerston must recollect, come to you and to the Queen, as well as to himself.'

Ever since the Reform Act of 1832 the Whigs had been increasingly, if unwillingly, dependent on the votes of the growing Radical group. Roebuck, one of the latter, described the Whigs as 'an exclusive and aristocratic faction, though at times employing democratic principles and phrases as weapons of offence against their opponents ... When out of office they are demagogues; in power they become exclusive oligarchs.' The election of 1847 left Russell dependent either on the Radicals or on the Peelites for a majority.

British party politics entered in 1846 on a period of flux and confusion which was to last for most of the remainder of the Prince's life. The Protectionists were numerous and well disciplined, but lacked maturity, and the Queen and Prince dreaded their return to power for the havoc they might wreak at home. On the other hand,

(opposite)
Sir Joseph Paxton (1803–1865)
Engraving by S. W. Reynolds after the painting by Octavius Oakley, published 1 May 1851 (British Museum)

After working for several years in various gardens, Joseph Paxton was invited by the sixth Duke of Devonshire to become his head gardener at Chatsworth in 1826. Paxton accepted and in January 1827 married Sarah Bown, the housekeeper's niece and daughter of a Matlock mill-owner. Encouraged by the Duke, Paxton re-organized the gardens at Chatsworth on a lavish scale to include the Great Conservatory, the Emperor Fountain and the Lily House, which inspired his design for the Crystal Palace. Loyal to the Duke, Paxton declined Prince Albert's invitation to reconstruct the miserably neglected gardens at Windsor, eventually becoming the Duke's agent and financial adviser and travelling with him extensively on the Continent.

In addition to writing books and editing magazines on horticulture, Paxton made a considerable fortune as a railway speculator. He had over twenty years experience in building glass structures when he embarked on designing the Crystal Palace, for which he was knighted in 1851. Paxton subsequently organized the removal and re-erection of the Crystal Palace at Sydenham.

After the Duke of Devonshire's death in 1858, Paxton relinquished his post at Chatsworth, and for the next seven years busied himself as Member of Parliament for Coventry. He died at Sydenham in 1865 and was buried at Edensor, the model village he had helped to create.

---

the alternative of rule by the Whig magnates had never been congenial to Albert, and Palmerston's policy, a combination of revolution abroad and standstill at home, was highly repugnant to him. The Radicals, divided between the 'Peace Party' and ultra-Palmerstonian nationalism, had little to attract him. Only Peel and his disciples, Aberdeen and Gladstone, enjoyed his full confidence, but they would not serve under Russell or Stanley.

The general election of 1847 showed clearly that the country had turned its back on Protection and now Disraeli, having achieved leadership of the Protectionist Tories under the nominal suzerainty of Lord Stanley, sought to dissociate his party from this policy. While many Protectionists denounced the Great Exhibition of 1851, the 'unwholesome castle of glass', as encouraging the entry of foreign products, Disraeli described it as an enchanted pile raised by 'the sagacious taste and the prescient philanthropy of an accomplished and enlightened Prince'.

In 1843 Prince Albert had succeeded the Duke of Sussex as President of the Royal Society. Spurred on by the success of exhibitions of manufactures and decorative art sponsored by the Society, Prince Albert was anxious to reach out to a far greater public than could be affected by purely national displays. He was therefore ready to respond to the promptings of Henry Cole, fresh from his visit with Digby Wyatt to the French national fair of 1849, that an exhibition should be organized which would be international in scope. A royal commission was appointed in January 1850 with Prince Albert as chairman. He had the full backing of Peel, who, apart from his interest in the arts, realized that, in an ever expanding industrial society, stability would best be achieved through the creation of wealth. Aware as Prince Albert was that the distances which separated the different nations were rapidly receding before the achievements of modern invention, he hoped that the Great Exhibition would be a symbol not only of social but also of political reconciliation. But first, the Prince's 'rubbishy Exhibition' as King Ernest of Hanover described it, had to undergo 'its ordeal of doubt, discussion, even opposition' before the workers 'like swarms of bees among the trees' could commence building the great glass edifice. As King Leopold wrote to Queen Victoria, 'Abuse is somewhat *the staff of life in England*, everything, everybody is to be abused', and Prince Albert met the full blast of hostile criticism, being told at one stage to pack out of London with his nuisance to the Isle of Dogs! The choice of site and the style of building raised innumerable difficulties, whilst the unexpected death of Peel in July 1850 was a shattering blow to his faithful disciple. However, Hyde Park was agreed on, and Paxton came to the rescue with his Crystal Palace. On 1 May 1851, the Queen was able to record that the opening ceremony 'was a thousand times superior' to her coronation, 'the enthusiasm and cheering too were much more touching, for in a church naturally all is silent.'

From start to finish the exhibition was an overwhelming success and a personal triumph for Prince Albert. His modest comment, 'quite satisfactory', fell far short of the loud appraisal of the thousands who flocked to marvel at the multifarious British and foreign exhibits recorded for posterity in the *Official Descriptive and Illustrated Catalogue* published as the exhibition was about to close. If ingenuity supplanted taste and the keynote of manufactures was often quantity rather than quality, nevertheless the group of buildings, housing technological schools and institutes and the Victoria and Albert Museum, erected eventually at South Kensington on land purchased from funds arising out of the exhibition, went a long way towards fulfilling Prince Albert's aim to further the influence of the arts and sciences, and in his words to 'ensure that the Great Exhibition of 1851 should not become a transitory event of mere temporary interest'.

By the time the exhibition ended Prince Albert had not only convinced certain distinguished foreign visitors that liberal views could achieve practical results, but had, as far as the French were concerned, eliminated the spectacle of 'prejudice walking to and fro in flesh and blood' and paved the way for the realization of Louis Philippe's earlier dream of an *entente cordiale*.

(*below*)
The Royal Commissioners for the Great Exhibition of 1851
Painting by Henry Wyndham Phillips
(Victoria and Albert Museum)

The Prince, seated, studies plans for the elevation of the building, whilst Joseph Paxton, his hands on the table, looks on from the Prince's right. Seated half-facing the Prince are Lord Derby on his left and William Cubitt on his right, while Lord John Russell and Sir Robert Peel are behind him. Henry Cole stands third from the far left.

The Great Exhibition 83

(*opposite*)
The Opening of the Great Exhibition, 1851
Painting by Henry Courtney Selous (Victoria and Albert Museum)

The Chinese man in front was not in fact an official, but a 'stray Celestial friend', who, during the singing of the Hallelujah Chorus, came forward with perfect composure and made a deep obeisance to the Queen.

1 Her Majesty the Queen
2 His Royal Highness Prince Albert, K.G., F.R.S., etc., etc., President of the Royal Commission
3 His Royal Highness the Prince of Wales
4 Her Royal Highness the Princess Royal
5 Her Royal Highness the Duchess of Kent
6 Her Royal Highness Princess Mary of Cambridge
7 His Royal Highness the Duke of Cambridge
8 Her Grace the Duchess of Sutherland, Mistress of the Robes
9 The Hon. Miss Flora Macdonald, Maid of Honour to Her Majesty
10 The Marchioness of Douro, Lady in Waiting on Her Majesty
11 The Hon. Miss Seymour, Maid of Honour to Her Majesty
12 Her Royal Highness the Princess of Prussia
13 Lord William Paulett, Equerry to the Duke of Cambridge
14 The Most Noble the Marquess of Breadalbane, Lord Chamberlain
15 His Grace the Archbishop of Canterbury
16 Field Marshal His Grace the Duke of Wellington, K.G., Commander in Chief
17 Field Marshal the Marquess of Anglesea, K.G., Master General of the Ordnance
18 The Rt. Hon. Lord John Russell, M.P., F.R.S., Royal Commissioner
19 The Rt. Hon. the Earl of Derby, Royal Commissioner
20 The Rt. Hon. the Earl Granville, Royal Commissioner, Chairman of the Committee for Communicating with Local Committees
21 Sir William Cubitt, F.R.S., President of Institution of Civil Engineers, Royal Commissioner, and Member of the Building Committee. Knighted by Her Majesty for his services to the Exhibition
22 Samuel Morton Peto, Esq., Member of the Finance Committee
23 C. Wentworth Dilke, Esq., Member of the Executive Committee
24 Lieut. Col. Reid, R.E., K.C.B., F.R.S., Chairman of the Executive Committee. Raised to the rank of Knight Commander of the Bath for his services
25 Henry Cole, Esq., C.B., Member of the Executive Committee. Created a Companion of the Order of the Bath for his services
26 Owen Jones, R.A., Superintendent of the Decoration of the Building and Exhibition generally
27 Sir Charles Fox, C.E., of the Firm of Fox and Henderson, Contractors for the erection of the Building. Knighted by Her Majesty for his services
28 Sir Joseph Paxton, Designer of the Exhibition Building. Knighted by Her Majesty on account of his services
29 Sir Stafford Henry Northcote, Bart., Secretary to the Royal Commission
30 Edgar A. Bowring, Esq., Assistant Secretary to the Royal Commission
31 J. Scott Russell, Esq., F.R.S., Secretary to the Royal Commission
32 Dr. Lyon Playfair, F.R.S., Special Commissioner to communicate with Local Committees
33 Lieut. Col. J. A. Lloyd, F.R.S., Special Commissioner to communicate with Local Committees
34 Thomas Bazley, Esq., Royal Commissioner
35 John Gott, Esq., Royal Commissioner
36 Richard Cobden, Esq., M.P., Royal Commissioner
37 The Rt. Hon. Lord Overstone, Royal Commissioner
38 Matthew Digby Wyatt, Esq., Secretary to the Executive Committee
39 C. H. Wild, Esq., Engineering Superintendent of the Works
40 George Drew, Esq., Member of the Executive Committee
41 Robert Stephenson, Esq., M.P., F.R.S., Royal Commissioner
42 Charles Barry, Esq., (Sir Charles), R.A., F.R.S., Royal Commissioner
43 The Rt. Hon. William Ewart Gladstone, M.P., Royal Commissioner
44 Francis Fuller, Esq., Member of the Executive Committee
45 Mr. Henderson, of the Firm of Fox and Henderson, Contractors for the Building
46 Thomas Field Gibson, Esq., Royal Commissioner
47 The Rt. Hon. Henry Labouchere, M.P., Royal Commissioner
48 The Rt. Hon. the Earl of Carlisle
49 Capt. Shepherd, Chairman of the Hon. East India Company, Royal Commissioner
50 Mr. Belshaw, Receiver of British Goods
51 Sir Charles Lyell, F.R.S., Royal Commissioner
52 Sir Charles Lock Eastlake, P.R.A., F.R.S., Royal Commissioner
53 Sir Richard Westmacott, R.A., Royal Commissioner
54 Mr. George Wallis, Superintendent of Classes 11, 12, 13, 14, 15, 18, 20, and of Juries
55 Lieut. Ducane, R.E., Assistant Superintendent of Foreign side
56 Henry Hensman, C.E., Superintendent of the Machinery department
57 [*unknown*]
58 Lieut. Crossman, R.E., Assistant in the arrangement of the space and admission of articles
59 Lieut. Tyler, R.E., Superintendent of the Colonial, Chinese, and Persian departments
60 The Chinaman Hee Sing, who happened to be present on the occasion
61 His Excellency Abbott Lawrence, Ambassador from the United States of America
62 M. Sallendronze de Lamornaire, French Commissioner
63 Chevalier de Burg, Austrian Commissioner
64 Capt. Owen, R.E., Superintendent of the Foreign side of the Building
65 Von Viebahu, Privy Finance Councillor, Commissioner for the Zollverein
66 Edward Zohrab, Esq., Consul from the Ottoman Port in London, and Turkish Commissioner
67 M. Gabriel de Kamenshi, Russian Commissioner
68 His Excellency M. Sylvain Van de Weyer, Belgium Minister
69 Charles Tottie, Esq., Consul and Commissioner for Sweden and Norway
70 Sy. Hamda Elmkadden, Tunisian Commissioner
71 Don Manuel de Ysasi, Spanish Commissioner
72 M. Tresca, Superintendent of the French Department
73 Professor Colladen, Swiss Commissioner
74 Charles Buschek, Esq., Austrian Commissioner
75 W. E. Logan, Esq., Director of Provincial Geological Survey, Canadian Commissioner
76 The Rt. Hon. Lord Viscount Canning, Chairman of Juries, etc., etc.
77 Sir Henry T. De la Beche, C.B., F.R.S., Member of Committee of Sections, and Chairman of Jury, Class 1
78 Philip Pusey, Esq., M.P., F.R.S., Royal Commissioner, and Chairman of Jury, Class 9
79 W. Fairbairn, Esq., Juror, Class 5
80 Lieut. Ward, R.E., Secretary to the Committee of Chairmen and Juries
81 Dr. Wylde, Juror, Class 10
82 Thomas Wentworth, Esq., Juror, Class 13
83 Warren De la Rue, Esq., F.R.S., F.C.S., Juror, Class 29
84 Wm. Filkin, Esq., Mayor of Nottingham, and Chairman of Jury, Class 22
85 R. L. Chance, Esq., Juror, Class 24, and Manufacturer of the Glass of which the Building was constructed
86 Sir David Brewster, F.R.S., Chairman of Jury, Class 10
87 Thomas De la Rue, Esq., Juror, Class 17
88 Dr. Arnott, F.R.S., Juror, Class 7
89 Barm M. d'Ostries, Juror, Class 9
90 His Royal Highness the Prince Frederick William of Prussia
91 His Royal Highness the Prince of Prussia
92 His Royal Highness Prince Edward of Saxe-Weimar
93 The Hon. Col. Seymour, Equerry to H.R.H. Prince Albert
94 His Grace the Duke of Devonshire
95 The Countess of Grosvenor
96 Her Grace the Duchess of Argyle
97 His Grace the Duke of Argyle

The Great Exhibition 85

Sir Henry Cole (1808–1882)
Painting by Samuel Laurence, 1865
(National Portrait Gallery)

Henry Cole, distinguished for his bustling, almost overwhelming energy, was, like Paxton, a man of many parts. He became one of four senior assistant keepers appointed when the Record Office was established in 1838 and was later partly responsible for the erection of the building in Fetter Lane. He was working at a branch of the Record Office in the riding school at Carlton House when Prince Albert came there in 1842 in search of furniture previously owned by George IV. The Prince was very impressed by the methodical way in which Cole was classifying the mass of records stored there and again in 1849 by Cole's attractive display of guidebooks and other material in the royal train conveying Prince Albert to lay the foundation stone of Grimsby docks.

Cole studied watercolour under David Cox and learned to etch. He issued a series of children's books under the title of *Felix Summerly's Home Treasury*, designed the first Christmas card and helped Rowland Hill to launch the penny post. In 1845 Cole's design for a tea service won the award offered by the Society of Arts, of which Prince Albert had been president since 1843. He was elected a member of the society and became its chairman in 1851 and 1852. One of his principal aims was the promotion of exhibitions, and thus he became a member of the executive committee set up by the royal commission appointed in 1850 to plan the Great Exhibition of 1851. Cole worked in close cooperation with the Prince, and at the end of the exhibition was made a Commander of the Order of the Bath. In October 1851 Cole was offered the secretaryship of the School of Design, reconstituted in 1852 as the Department of Practical Art and in 1853 as the Department of Science and Art, of which Cole and Dr. Lyon Playfair were joint secretaries. Playfair retired in 1858, and Cole resigned in 1873.

Cole played an important part in assembling the collections which went to form the Victoria and Albert Museum and in the erection of buildings on the site acquired by the royal commissioners with funds accruing from the Great Exhibition.

(opposite top)
Entry of Queen Victoria and Prince Albert into Paris, 18 August 1855
Watercolour by Adolphe Bayot and Adrien Dauzats (Royal Collection) *see chapter six*

Queen Victoria was the first reigning British monarch to visit Paris since the infant Henry VI was crowned there in 1430. She arrived by train at the Gare de l'Est and drove by way of the new Boulevard de Strasbourg, the Madeleine, Place de la Concorde and Champs-Elysées to Saint-Cloud. 'We entered a carriage with four horses, Vicky and I sitting together... the Emperor and Albert opposite... No description can give an idea of the whole scene. Paris is the most beautiful and the gayest of cities with its high handsome houses... decorated in the most tasteful manner possible, with banners, flags, arches, flowers, inscriptions and finally illuminations; the windows full of people up to the tops of the houses... and everybody most enthusiastic... There were endless cries of "Vive la Reine d'Angleterre", "Vive l'Empereur", "Vive le Prince Albert".' Thus the Queen described it in her journal. Bismarck, undoubtedly piqued as a Russophile, described the Queen's reception as cool, with the enthusiasm restricted to the English side. The procession is here shown passing the Porte Saint-Denis with the Porte Saint-Martin in the background.

(opposite bottom)
Supper in the Salle de Spectacle, Versailles, 25 August 1855
Watercolour by Eugène Lami (Royal Collection) *see chapter six*

Prince Albert was fully conscious of the historic past surrounding that evening at Versailles. 'So numerous were the strange impressions wrought by the contrast of past with present that one could often only wonder. Thus we supped at Versailles in the theatre where the Gardes du Corps held their famous banquet, and even sat in the box in which Marie Antoinette showed herself to them,' he wrote to King Leopold (29 August). Four hundred people sat down to supper at forty small tables of ten each, reported the Queen.

Prince Albert's letter referred to events in 1789 when the Régiment de Flandre arrived at Versailles to join the Gardes du Corps in defending the King, and the officers of the Gardes gave a banquet on 1 October to the Flanders officers. Abundant toasts to the King and Queen were drunk, but none to the Nation. Louis XVI and Marie Antoinette appeared to receive the applause of the officers, while the tricolour cockade was said to have been trampled on. When this report reached Paris, a mob of women, incensed, marched to Versailles and forced the King and Queen to return to Paris on 6 October. Henceforth they were prisoners and King and Assembly were at the mercy of the Paris mob.

86 *The Great Exhibition*

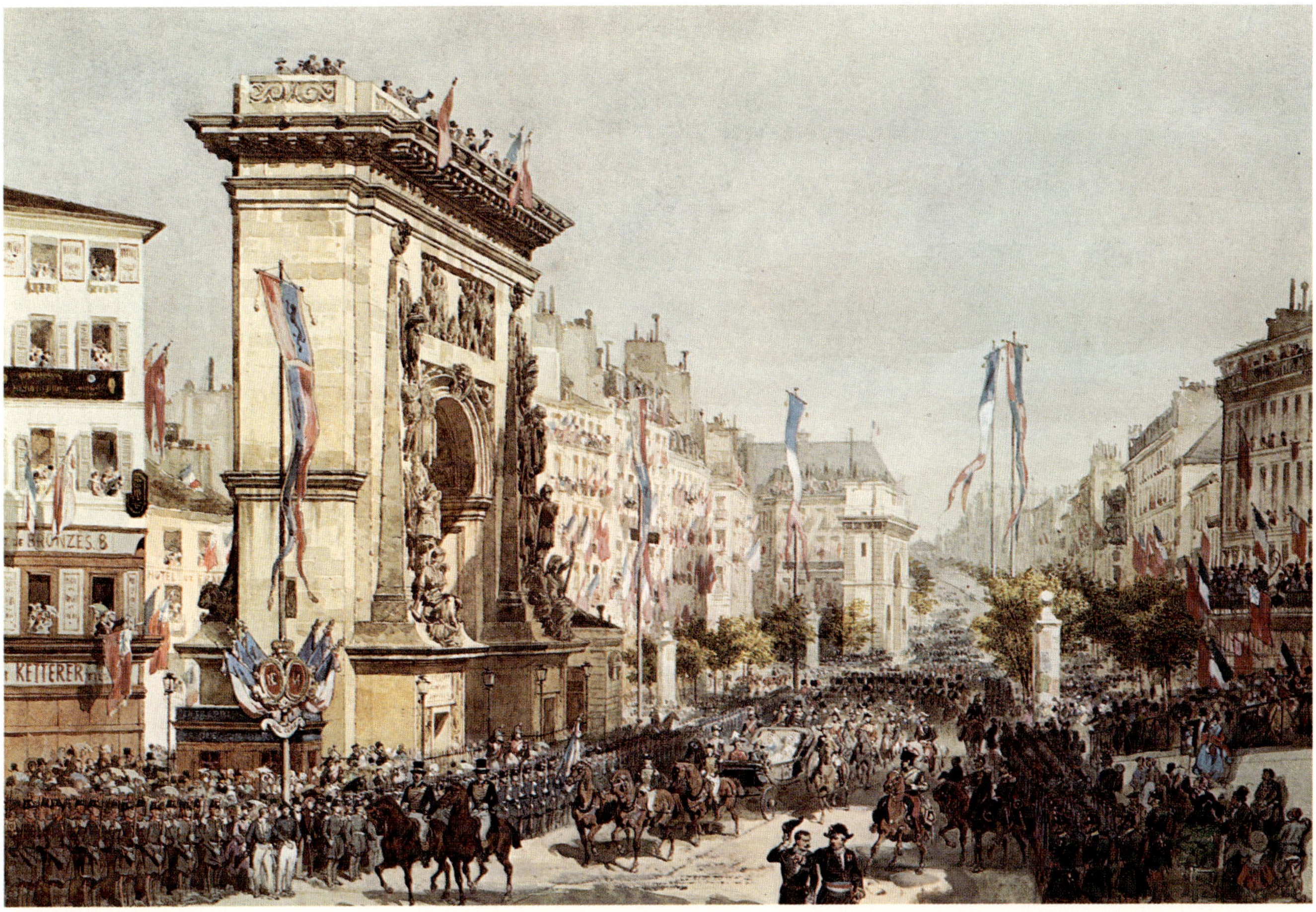
BRONZES B
KETTERER

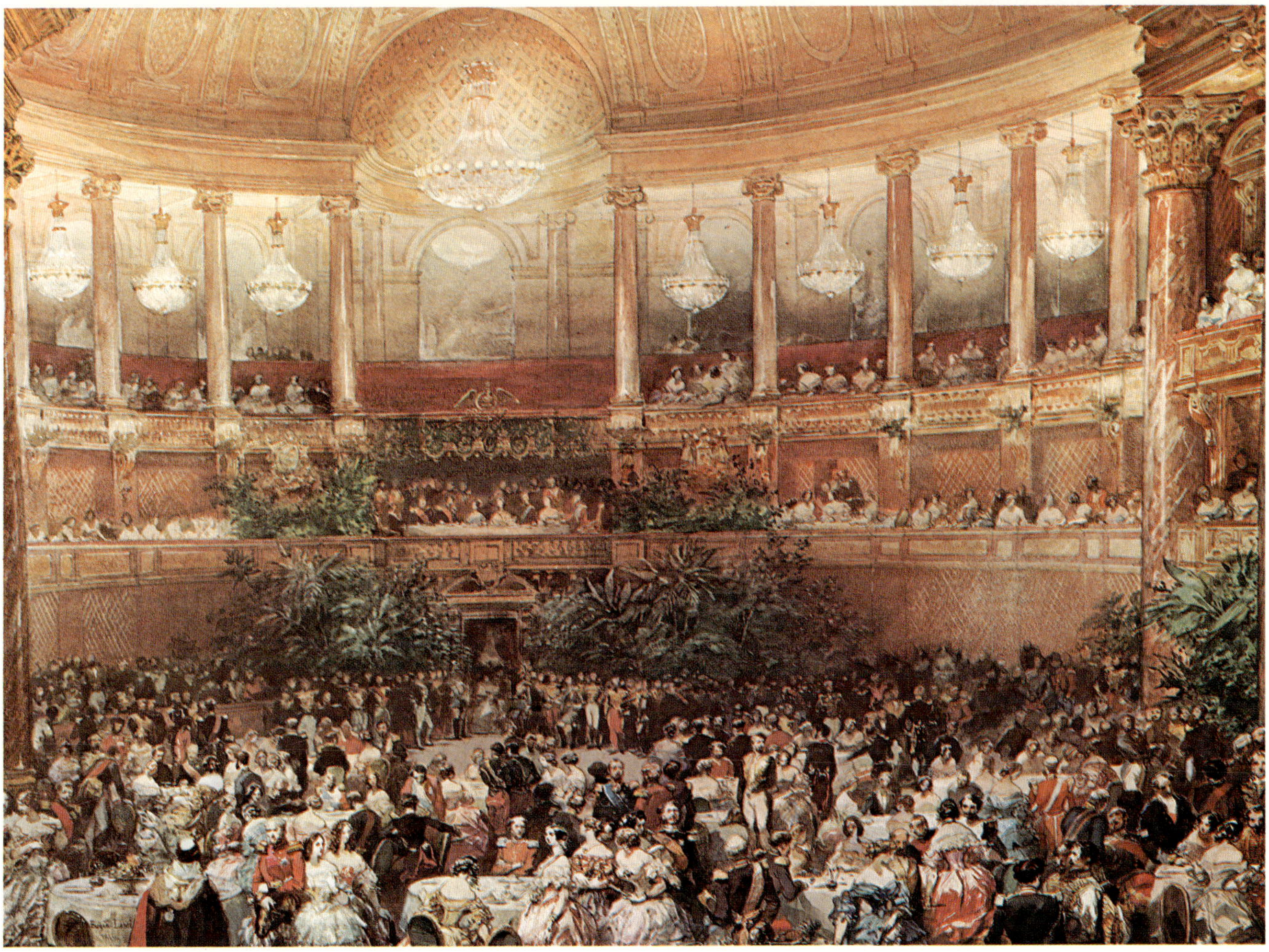

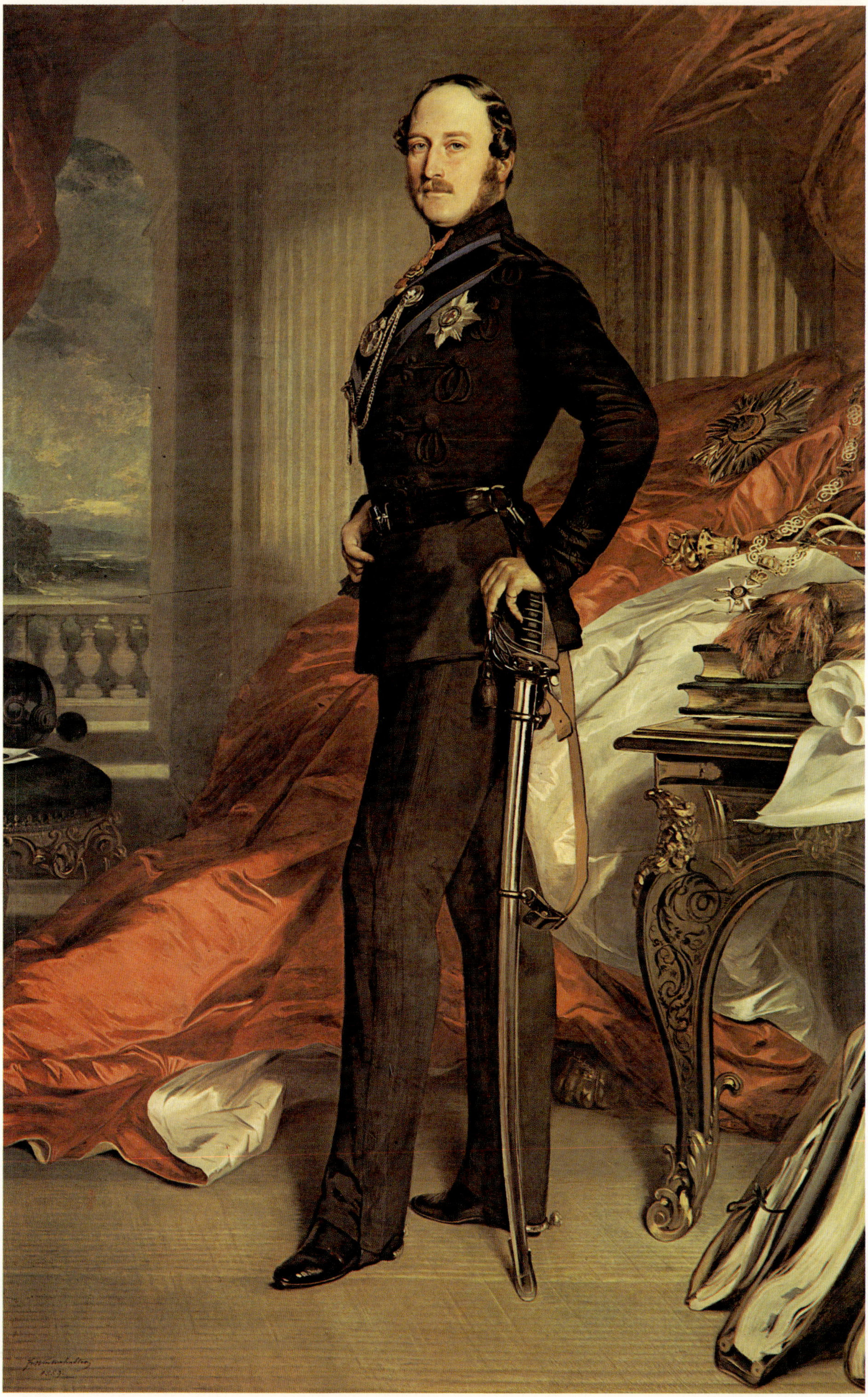

(*opposite*)
The Prince Consort in the Uniform of Colonel-in-Chief of the Rifle Brigade
Painting by Franz Xaver Winterhalter (Royal Collection)

On 25 June 1857 the Privy Council ordered that Prince Albert should henceforward be known under the newly created title of 'Prince Consort'. It was a source of regret to the Queen that this should not have been done by Act of Parliament.

This last portrait done from life in May 1859 was commissioned by the Queen. It depicts the Prince after the birth of his first grandchild and immediately before the decisive battles of Napoleon III's Italian war against Austria. This led to a course of events in Germany which were to cause the Prince increasing worry during his last years and to contribute to his early death.

(*below*)
The Great Exhibition: View across the Transept
Lithograph by Joseph Nash (Victoria and Albert Museum)

One of the problems facing the building committee was how to preserve the fine old elms occupying part of the exhibition site. This was finally solved by Joseph Paxton, who, accepting the idea of a transept, which had been suggested at a late stage in the building plans, conceived the brilliant notion of covering the transept with a vaulted and not a flat roof, so that the trees could be accommodated centrally within the structure.

H.R.H. Prince Albert
Medal struck by J. Taylor, London, inside the Crystal Palace, 1851 (M. Scheele)

The Machinery Courts at the Great Exhibition fascinated the Queen, who recorded in her journal that she had seen 'medals made by machinery, which not more than 15 years ago were made by hand, 50 million instead of *one* million can be supplied in a week now.'

Medal
Issued to Commemorate the Great Exhibition of 1851 (British Museum)

The Great Exhibition 89

Prince Albert's Season Ticket
(Victoria and Albert Museum)

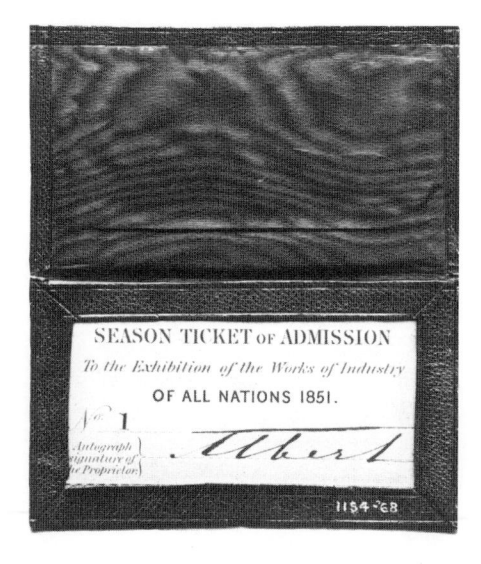

90 *The Great Exhibition*

The Crystal Palace and Park, Sydenham
Lithograph by J. Needham after a painting by J. D. Harding, 1854 (Victoria and Albert Museum)

In accordance with the original agreement, the Great Exhibition building had to be dismantled and a new site found before 1 June 1852. Paxton would have liked it to be retained in Hyde Park as a 'Winter Park and Garden under glass', maintaining that its removal would be uneconomic and an act of vandalism. However, Prince Albert was opposed to the idea and in April 1852 Parliament voted for its removal.

Paxton had already taken steps to re-erect it on a new site. On 17 May 1852 the newly formed Crystal Palace Company, of which Paxton was a director, published its prospectus. The Hyde Park building was purchased, and, in line with Paxton's flair for railway speculation, a site with rail access was selected. This comprised the grounds of Penge Place, southeast of London, owned by L. Schuster, a director of the new company and also of the London, Brighton and South Coast Railway, together with an adjoining estate. Another link with railway interests was the appointment of Samuel Laing, chairman of the Brighton Railway, as chairman of the new company. Paxton was nominated director of the winter garden, park and conservatory, whilst Matthew Digby Wyatt became director of works and Owen Jones director of decorations. Various alterations and additions were made to the original Crystal Palace, and the new, more grandiose building proved very costly to erect. It was opened by Queen Victoria on 10 June 1854 and enjoyed great success for over half a century as a popular cultural and recreational centre. The building was destroyed by fire on 30 November 1936.

Faraday Lecturing at the Royal Institution before Prince Albert and the Prince of Wales, 1855
After a lithograph by Alexander Blaikley (National Portrait Gallery, owned by the Royal Institution)

Prince Albert, who, in his inaugural address as president of the British Association in 1859, described himself as merely 'a simple admirer and would-be student of Science', took a great interest in scientific achievements. He was extremely anxious that science, 'until of late almost systematically excluded from our school and university education', should receive proper recognition and encouragement from the state.

Michael Faraday (1791–1867), famous for his experiments in electromagnetism, always had a great respect for his audience and was at his best when lecturing to young people. A man of strong religious conviction, Faraday believed that religion and science should be kept apart. After an earlier misunderstanding, Lord Melbourne finally persuaded Faraday to accept a pension. Queen Victoria, doubtless at the instigation of the Prince, placed a small house on the green at Hampton Court at Faraday's disposal. There he died in August 1867.

The Great Exhibition

Henry John Temple, third Viscount Palmerston (1784–1865)
Painting by John Partridge, 1844/45 (National Portrait Gallery)

'Hat der Teufel einen Sohn
so heisst er sicher Palmerston'
('If the Devil has a son
His name is surely Palmerston')

Prince Albert shared to the full this widespread German view of the man who was Foreign Secretary under Earl Grey, Lord Melbourne and Lord John Russell for fifteen years between 1830 and 1851. In September 1854 at Saint-Omer the Prince explained to Napoleon III that Palmerston's foreign policy was founded on Canning's thesis of forming a counterpoise to the Holy Alliance led by Russia, by supporting in every country popular parties aiming at establishing a constitution on the British model. Prince Albert pointed out that if such a pro-British party were worsted, this would incur defeat and discredit for the British government, while in the event of success it would have to prove its independence by taking measures hurtful to Britain. The consequent detestation of Palmerston by Continental governments roused British national indignation in his favour, giving him great popularity, which he exploited to coerce his colleagues and the Queen, while resistance to his policies could be stigmatized as truckling to European combinations against him.

Palmerston was insularly impervious to the danger from such revolutionary movements to rulers linked by close ties of blood or friendship to the Queen. He supported national unity in Italy and opposed it in Germany, while Prince Albert took the inverse views. The clash was exacerbated by royal dissatisfaction with Palmerston's often impetuous methods. He believed in firm, clear championship of British interests. 'Let them see you are able and determined to repel force by force'.

Never a true Whig, he became the 'new opposition leader', according to Sir James Graham, on his dismissal by Russell in 1851. His opposition to further Parliamentary reform brought him closer to the Tories, and he refused office under Derby three times in 1852. Prince Albert was particularly suspicious of a rapprochement between Palmerston and Disraeli 'considering the *laxity of the political consciences* which both these gentlemen have hitherto exhibited'.

Palmerston served as Home Secretary under Aberdeen and when that government fell was called in to save the situation. He was Prime Minister from 1855 until his death except for the brief Derby government of 1858–59. He was by then better regarded at court and was awarded the Garter in 1856.

92 The Great Exhibition

Lord John Russell, later first Earl Russell (1792–1878)
Engraving by James Fade after a painting by Sir Francis Grant (British Museum)

A younger son of the sixth Duke of Bedford, Lord John Russell became a Member of Parliament in 1813 and soon devoted himself to the cause of Parliamentary reform. His family origins and career fully justified the Peelite Sir James Graham's dictum, 'The title of Whig is Lord John's distinctive appellation. . . To un-Whig Ld. John Russell is like the unfrocking of a Parson.' He won nationwide popularity when he introduced the First Reform Bill in the House of Commons in March 1831 and again after its endorsement by the electors in June. He emphasized the impossibility that 'the whisper of a faction should prevail against the voice of a nation'. Under the premiership of Lord Melbourne he became leader of the Whigs in the Commons and was accepted by both Radicals and Irish.

Following the fall of Peel Lord John became Prime Minister in July 1846 with Palmerston as Foreign Secretary, 'those two dreadful old men,' as Queen Victoria sighed. This was the period of greatest friction between the Queen and Prince on the one hand and the government on the other over Italy, Schleswig-Holstein, Spain and Portugal. Lord John tried vainly to curb Palmerston and was finally obliged to dismiss him in December 1851 after his precipitate recognition of Louis Napoleon's *coup d'état*. This caused a personal rift and rivalry between Russell and Palmerston which undermined the unity of the Whig Party whose exclusive and dynastic principles were by then discredited.

Russell agreed to serve under Palmerston in 1855 and again as Foreign Secretary in his Liberal government of 1859–65. In this capacity he accompanied the Queen and Prince Albert to Coburg in 1860. Created Earl Russell in 1861, he succeeded Palmerston as Prime Minister in 1865–66. He was the last of the Whigs. 'Lord John may do what he pleases; but he will be called a Whig to the end of his life,' said Lord Aberdeen.

The Great Exhibition

THE ALLIANCE POLKA,
COMPOSED BY
C.H.R. MARRIOTT.
Ent. Sta. Hall.
Pr. 2/6.
LONDON, B. WILLIAMS, 11, PATERNOSTER ROW & 170, Gt DOVER Rd
WHERE MAY BE HAD BY SAME AUTHOR
THE SYREN'S SCHOTTISCHE 2/. _ AUTUMN LEAVES, WALTZES 3/. _ EUGENIE REDOWA, 2/.

The Crimean War, the French Alliance and Balmoral

The Great Exhibition of 1851 contributed to a dissipation of the mutual prejudices between England and France and so prepared the way for the close alliance which was to characterize the new decade. In France political uncertainties provided the occasion and the impetus for the *coup d'état* in December 1851 which gave absolute power to Louis Napoleon Bonaparte, who restored the Empire a year later. He was to bring fluidity to the international scene on which Albert's ambitions were concentrated and to dominate it for the remainder of the Prince's life.

Premature and hasty recognition of the *coup* by Palmerston provided the occasion for his dismissal by Russell with the full approval of the Queen and Prince, but the ensuing rift between the two Whig paladins increased yet more the fluidity of the British party political scene. Palmerston got his 'tit for tat with John Russell' within two months, and a Protectionist Tory government led by Derby, but dominated by the new meteor Disraeli, replaced it. Prince Albert disliked this government even more than Palmerston and feared a possible combination of the two. The defeat of Disraeli's budget, thanks to the oratory of the rising Peelite star Gladstone, initiated the duel of those Dioscuri of the high Victorian age. A coalition government under Lord Aberdeen, who enjoyed the Prince's complete confidence, included both Peelites and Whigs and was the first step towards the emergence of the Gladstonian Liberal party.

But the new government was soon faced by a crisis over Russian threats to the Turkish empire. Napoleon III saw a chance to break the logjam of the treaties of 1815 which constrained France and had successfully weathered the upsurge of nationalities in 1848–49. He sought to break the Waterloo alliance and link Britain ever closer to France. Austria inclined to the west, while Prussia was riven between a reactionary court subservient to Russia and the Liberal elements, led by the Prince of Prussia and Prince Albert's former mentor Bethmann-Hollweg, who looked to the west. It was a conflict between Russia and Europe.

Throughout 1853 the Russian threats to the Turkish empire grew and while an Anglo-French fleet assembled outside the Dardanelles, Russian forces invaded Turkey's tributary principalities on the Danube. The Turks declared war in October and their warships were sunk at Sinope. Britain's and France's fleets entered the Black Sea in January 1854 and they drifted into the Crimean War against Russia in March. Fears for British trading interests and resentment against the Tsar's rôle as a suppressor of revolution in 1848–49 combined to rouse British feeling against him, so that Sinope was described as a massacre.

Although Leopold of Coburg had been a Russian protégé when he wooed Princess Charlotte, he had lost all favour with the Tsar and his manifold clients at the German courts by accepting the Belgian crown. It was a supreme irony and injustice therefore that in 1853 as British opinion, led by Palmerston and whipped up by the Radicals, became ever more anti-Russian, Albert should have been denounced as a Russian agent, largely on the grounds that he was a German prince. 'The most absurd reports are rife concerning Prince Albert, and are believed by the public, even to that of his being sent to the Tower for unconstitutional practices,' wrote Lord Malmesbury, Derby's Foreign Secretary (15 January 1854). Time would do him justice, continued Malmesbury, 'And convince the world that no sovereign could have at his side a better counsellor, removed as he is from all personal disputes of parties.' His information

(*opposite*)
Queen Victoria and Napoleon III
Titlepage of *The Alliance Polka*, music composed by C. H. R. Marriott, 1855
(British Museum)

on the courts of northern Europe was invaluable 'as being out of reach of our diplomats'.

The summer of 1854 was wasted by the allied forces on the Bulgarian coast and they only landed in the Crimea in September with a view to taking the great Russian base at Sebastopol. But winter was upon them on the open ground before the fortress could be attacked. Parliamentary parsimony and administrative incompetence subjected the troops to terrible privations relieved only by the ministrations of Florence Nightingale and her team of nurses.

In January 1855 the House of Commons voted by a large majority for a commission of inquiry into the condition of the Army and the supply services. Aberdeen was a 'peace' and not a 'war' Premier and so, like Asquith to Lloyd George and Chamberlain to Churchill, he resigned to give place to the more dynamic Palmerston, fresh from a visit to the French Emperor, whose support he enjoyed. The same year saw the apogee of the French alliance in the cordial exchange of visits between the Emperor and the Queen with its culminating moments at Les Invalides and Versailles.

To Queen Victoria the most significant event of her journey to Paris was probably her visit on 24 August to the tomb of Napoleon I at Les Invalides. It was fifteen years since the prince de Joinville had escorted 'les Cendres' back from St. Helena. 'There I stood, at the arm of Napoleon III, his nephew, before the coffin of England's bitterest foe; I, the granddaughter of that King who hated him most ... and this very nephew ... being my nearest and dearest ally! The organ of the church was playing "God Save the Queen"... It seems as if in this tribute of respect to a departed foe, old enmities were wiped out, and the seal of Heaven placed upon that bond of unity ... between two great and powerful nations,' the Queen wrote in her journal.

'After a moment of meditation, of absolute silence, the Queen with a respectful, calm and severe expression, turned to the Prince of Wales and putting her hand on his shoulder said "Kneel down before the tomb of the great Napoleon" ... Waterloo, St. Helena ... the English alliance ... England in the person of her Queen and of her future King who was kneeling before the remains of Napoleon: all that made my senses reel.' Thus Marshal Canrobert, hero of the Crimea and veteran of Algeria, recorded the episode in his memoirs.

That moment was supremely significant in the context of the previous half century and of the first half of the next century, when England's course was to be set by that kilted boy whose visit to Paris as Prince of Wales made him for life a friend of France. In between, however, was to come the aftermath of an encounter by his father with Bismarck next evening at Versailles.

After the victory over Russia the paths of England and France began to diverge again. Italian exiles in London plotted to murder the Emperor and Palmerston's attempt to smooth over the crisis led to his fall in 1858. The second Derby-Disraeli government was less obnoxious to the Queen and Prince than the first. Moreover its attitude towards Napoleon III's Italian war against Austria was more aligned to that of the court than were Palmerston's and Russell's. The Prince feared that Germany might be drawn in and that Napoleon might seize the Rhine. Albert's neuralgic point was touched.

The Queen took with her to Paris a selection of official photographs of the war in the Crimea made by Roger Fenton, first secretary of the London Photographic Society. In May 1853 she and Prince Albert, already well versed in the new art of photography, had become patrons of the recently formed Society to which they gave unstinted encouragement.

Prince Albert's greatest contribution to the application of photography lay characteristically in the field of art. As a distraction from his official duties he turned his attention early in 1853 to arranging the Raphael drawings in the royal collection. Assisted by Carl Ruland, his librarian at Windsor, the Prince undertook the monumental task of compiling, with the aid of photographic reproduction, a corpus of the entire artistic output of Raphael. As a guide he used J. D. Passavant's *Rafael von Urbino und sein Vater Giovanni Santi* (1839), which catalogued in detail every picture and drawing by Raphael. After Prince Albert's death Ruland completed the work at the Queen's request, and this pioneer work in art history, illustrated by photography, was published privately in 1876.

For Prince Albert the acquisition of Balmoral was more psychologically important than that of Osborne had been. In England he was never allowed to forget that he was a foreigner, worse still, a German! In Scotland he felt at one with the people, who, as he wrote to Duchess Caroline of Gotha, 'are more natural and marked by that honesty and sympathy which always distinguishes the inhabitants of mountainous countries, who live far away from towns.' Soothing as Osborne might be, its languorous charm could not compare with the severity and grandeur of the Highlands. Once the border was crossed both Queen Victoria and Prince Albert really entered into their own, sharing alike the satisfaction of a paternalistic relationship with their tenants at Balmoral unlike anything they had experienced in England. Excluded from inheriting the duchy of Coburg, Prince Albert created his own fief at Balmoral, and he was determined to make it as extensive as possible. He quickly assessed the advantages of possessing the neighbouring estates of Abergeldie and Birkhall, and, in addition, the vast forest of Ballochbuie, but Birkhall was the only one he managed to purchase outright in the name of the Prince of Wales. The fee simple of Balmoral was purchased in June 1852, but Prince Albert had to be content with the lease of

Abergeldie. Ballochbuie was not purchased until 1878. Later in 1852 the Queen received a totally unexpected bequest, a legacy of approximately £500,000 left to her 'for her sole use and benefit' by an eccentric and miserly barrister, John Camden Neild. Neild, who apparently never brushed his clothes for fear of destroying the nap and walked whenever possible when visiting his estates, was the second son of James Neild, the prison reformer. The news, which evidently cheered Stockmar in no ordinary degree, to the extent of wishing Mr. Neild a joyful resurrection, must have delighted even more Prince Albert and the Queen, about to create the new Balmoral with its improved cottages, stables, dairy and farm-buildings. It was to be a fitting abode where the Prince could climb, fish, shoot and meditate on the glories of the countryside, whilst the Queen, when not accompanying her husband, could indulge in all the cosier activities of a true *Landesmutter*.

Military Review in Windsor Great Park, 17 April 1855
Watercolour by G. H. Thomas (Royal Collection)

At 4 o'clock on a hot afternoon the royal party set off from Windsor Castle for the review of the Household troops in the Great Park, 'A most brilliant, and beautiful, and exciting affair... In the first carriage were the Empress (whom I always made get in and walk first), I, Bertie, Vicky and dear little Arthur; Albert, the Emperor, George [Duke of Cambridge] and all the military gentlemen on horseback... The crowd, in the Long Walk, of people on foot and horseback, was tremendous, and the excitement and cheering beyond description. They squeezed round the Emperor when we came to the gates, and rode across the grass where the review was to be, in such a way that I grew very nervous, as he rode along on a very fiery beautiful chestnut called "Philips" and was so exposed. He rides extremely well, and looks well on horseback, as he sits high... The enthusiasm, the crowd of excited people and riders, were quite indescribable. I never remember any excitement like it.' The Queen's description in her journal amply fits the scene depicted, 'the whole was quite a triumph'. Commanding the Horse Artillery was Lord Cardigan on the chestnut horse he had ridden as commander in the charge of the Light Brigade at Balaklava the previous year.

The Crimean War and Balmoral 97

98 *The Crimean War and Balmoral*

Napoleon III, Emperor of the French (1808–1873)
Lithograph by Léon Noel after a photograph by Mayer et Pierson (British Museum)

Louis Napoleon Bonaparte was the son of Louis Bonaparte, King of Holland, and Hortense de Beauharnais, the Empress Josephine's daughter by her first marriage. When Prince Leopold of Saxe-Coburg visited Paris he was befriended by Queen Hortense and he reciprocated this after Napoleon's defeat by obtaining for her from Tsar Alexander I a yearly pension of £16,000. With this she settled at Augsburg, where her finances were managed by Stockmar's brother Carl, and in Switzerland. Hardly suprisingly, her son Louis Napoleon grew up to speak French with a German accent and was well versed in German literature and song. He became the head of the Bonaparte dynasty on the death of his cousin the King of Rome in 1832.

Louis Napoleon was elected President of the French Republic by popular vote in December 1848 and confirmed himself in power by the *coup d'état* of December 1851, being proclaimed Emperor as Napoleon III in 1852. He regarded the duel with Britain as having been the cause of his uncle's ruin, determined on alliance rather than enmity with her. He sought to break up the European settlement of 1815 without incurring a renewal of the 'Waterloo Alliance' of Britain with Russia, Prussia and Austria which had imposed it and had checked Louis Philippe in Egypt and on the Rhine in 1840.

When Napoleon III visited England, in which he had formerly been an exile, in April 1855 the Queen was fascinated by this 'very *extraordinary*... almost... mysterious man. He is evidently possessed of indomitable courage, unflinching firmness of purpose, self-reliance, perseverance and great secrecy... how far he is actuated by a strong moral sense of right and wrong is difficult to say.' While King Louis Philippe had been '*thoroughly French* in character', 'the Emperor is as *unlike a Frenchman* as possible, being much more *German* than French in character.' This German aspect could certainly have helped towards an understanding with Prince Albert, although the value of a memorandum he wrote after visiting the Emperor at Saint-Omer in September 1854 'cannot be overstated; nor is it less valuable for the light which it throws upon the Prince's character, by the remarkable contrasts between himself and the Emperor of the French, which were elicited in the unreserved discussions which each seems equally to have courted,' wrote Sir Theodore Martin. The Emperor was reported by his ambassador to have spoken with enthusiasm of the Prince, 'saying that in all his experience he had never met with a person possessing such various and profound knowledge, or who communicated it with the same frankness... He had never learned so much in a short time.' Nevertheless the Prince always retained a certain suspicion of the Emperor's aims towards Germany, especially after his war against Austria in 1859.

Eugénie, Empress of the French (1826–1920)
Miniature by Sir William Ross (Royal Collection)

After his *coup d'état* in December 1851 the Prince-President confiscated all the properties of the House of Orléans in France. As an attack on property, this aroused considerable resentment among Europe's royal families and especially the Coburgs, some of whom, having married into the Orléans family, were affected.

When he became Emperor a year later, Napoleon sought the hand of Queen Victoria's niece, Adelaide of Hohenlohe-Langenburg. He was rebuffed and then married Eugénie de Montijo, descended from the Guzmáns, one of Spain's oldest and noblest families. Her sister, Paca, was married to the duque de Alba. Her father, a grandee of Spain, had been a progressive *afrancesado* in the Napoleonic period. Her mother was middle class, Scots and Belgian by descent, but rose for a time to be *camerera mayor* or Mistress of the Robes to Queen Isabella II. Eugénie's education in France, Spain and England was completely cosmopolitan. The family were close friends of Donoso Cortés, Spanish Minister in Paris and one of the clearest political analysts of his day. Eugénie was an auburn-haired beauty of outstanding charm and elegance speaking excellent English. 'The Empress is more beautiful than all the pictures which I have seen of her, uncommonly graceful and charming,' Bismarck wrote to his wife (27 August 1855).

When the Imperial couple visited England in April 1855 the Queen wrote to King Leopold, '*She* is very pleasing, very graceful and very unaffected, but very delicate. She *is* certainly very pretty and very uncommon-looking' (17 April 1855). She found her 'full of courage and spirit and yet so gentle'. 'The Empress Eugénie's manner was simple, and almost shy... throughout her visit she always kept behind the Queen, and the latter, who on several occasions with polite compliments made a show of letting the Empress go first, always ended by preceding her,' wrote Countess Bernstorff.

This was the beginning of a lifelong friendship which became ever deeper. The Empress had had one miscarriage and now the Queen was able to give her advice which facilitated the pregnancy she developed before the return visit to Paris. A bond of affection was created with the royal children, who wept at their departure from England, and especially with the Princess Royal and the Prince of Wales. Prince Albert 'got on famously with the Empress', wrote Queen Victoria, 'and so did I with the Emperor.' In fact the Prince was fascinated by Eugénie as by no other woman except the Queen.

The Crimean War and Balmoral 99

Medal
Issued to Commemorate the Comradeship in Arms of the British and French Armies in the Crimea (British Museum)

The obverse depicts a British guardsman and a French infantryman with flags and the words, 'The Holy Alliance—La Sainte Alliance'. The reverse is inscribed 'England and France united to defend the oppressed and avenge insulted Europe'. The Crimean War was seen in both countries as a struggle in defence of Europe and its values against Russian aggression.

Ball in the Galerie des Glaces, Versailles, 25 August 1855
Watercolour by Victor Chavet (Royal Collection)

The palace of Louis XIV at Versailles had not been used since Louis XVI and Marie Antoinette were carried off to Paris by the mob. Now for one evening the ancient splendours were revived by the Emperor for his British guests.

For the next half century especial significance, beyond anything he could have surmised, attached to one encounter by Prince Albert that evening. Among the guests was Otto von Bismarck, Prussian envoy to the Frankfurt Diet, in his white cuirassier's uniform, who was presented to the Queen and the Prince. 'The Prince, handsome and cool in his black uniform, conversed with me courteously, but in his manner there was a kind of malevolent curiosity from which I concluded that my anti-Western influence upon the King [of Prussia] was not unknown to him. In accordance with the mode of thought peculiar to him, he sought for the motives of my conduct not where they really lay, that is, in the anxiety to keep my country independent of foreign influences... In the eyes of the Prince... I was a reactionary party man who took up sides for Russia in order to further an absolutist and "Junker" policy... At that ball at Versailles Queen Victoria spoke to me in German. She gave me the impression of beholding in me a noteworthy but unsympathetic personality, but still her tone of voice was without that touch of ironical superiority that I thought I detected in Prince Albert's' (*Reflexions and Reminiscences*, vol. I, pp. 162–64). The Queen found him 'very Russian and Kreuzzeitung' [the reactionary Junker newspaper]. The contrasting colours of their uniforms might have seemed to Albert to represent the inverse of their views for Germany's future, for in face of this eccentric anachronistic Junker, representative of the reactionary militarist Prussian past, he felt confident that his own enlightened Liberalism represented Germany's future.

That same evening, the Princess Royal waltzed in the arms of the French Emperor. As she saw herself in the Hall of Mirrors the young girl, according to her biographer, Daphne Bennett, first became conscious of her own attractiveness. Within a month emotional fulfilment was to come in the person of the Prussian Prince who would be her fiancé. As she embarked on marriage, she could not know that it was the man in white, not the man in black, who would determine her future and ruin her own, her husband's and her father's dreams.

History was to be made twice more in the Galerie des Glaces: in 1871 when Bismarck's German Empire was proclaimed there in the palace dedicated to 'all the glories of France', and in 1919 when Clemenceau, the sworn enemy of Napoleon, consecrated the supreme humiliation of that German Empire.

100 The Crimean War and Balmoral

Medal
Issued to Commemorate the Visit of Napoleon III and the Empress Eugénie to England, April 1855 and that of Queen Victoria and Prince Albert to France, August 1855 (British Museum)

The medal depicts the British sovereign and consort on one side, the French couple on the other.

Otto von Bismarck (1815–1898)
Photograph by Jean Schaefer (British Museum)

If there was an arch-antagonist to Prince Albert's life and aims it was undoubtedly Otto von Bismarck who was to fulfil the Prince's dream in a manner he would have abhorred, to frustrate the lives of his chosen pupils, the Princess Royal and her husband, to debase the brother who had been his closest comrade, and finally to corrupt the grandson who at first seemed the guerdon of all Albert's ideals, so that he became the most loathed man in Victoria's realm and brought obloquy there for a generation on the name of German.

Prince Albert and Bismarck met only once, in the Hall of Mirrors at Versailles where Bismarck's German Empire was to be proclaimed in 1871 and to founder in 1919. A Junker or East Elbian squire, Bismarck was a leading member of the reactionary party in Prussia, who saw her future in alliance with the Russian despotism against the west. 'Prussians we are and Prussians we will remain,' was his motto for a German unity which was to be an extension of Prussian power. To him Albert was no Prussian and therefore had no right to interfere in Prussian policy. That he was a German was beside the point.

As Prussian envoy to the German Confederation at Frankfurt from 1851 to 1859, Bismarck opposed Austria in every way. On his 1855 visit to Paris he also met Napoleon III and was reassured by the impression that he was discreet and amiable but 'not so clever as the world esteems him . . . his understanding is overrated at the expense of his heart; he is at bottom good-natured, and has an unusual measure of gratitude for every service rendered him.' It was a shrewder analysis than any Prince Albert made and a decade later Bismarck was to exploit it ruthlessly.

The Crimean War and Balmoral 101

102 *The Crimean War and Balmoral*

Benjamin Disraeli (1804–1881)
Engraving by Sir Francis Grant, 1852 (British Museum)

Disraeli achieved early fame as a novelist. Prince Albert first met him in 1836 and dismissed him as 'a vain young Jew with Radical opinions'. He entered Parliament in 1837 as a Conservative, but was refused office by Peel in 1841. When Peel, with the support of most of his cabinet, adopted Free Trade in 1846 and passed the necessary legislation with Whig and Radical support, Disraeli led the attack on him in the Commons with a new style of oratory, cool, mocking and oblique. The party which Peel had rebuilt after the Reform Act of 1832 was divided between a Peelite élite and the mass of Protectionist backbenchers. After a brief interlude under Lord George Bentinck, the latter in 1848 elected Disraeli as their leader in the Commons and he became the architect of a revived Conservative Party.

With his strong admiration for Peel, Prince Albert regarded the Protectionists as immature and had a strong distrust of Disraeli, whom he regarded as untruthful and possessed of a lax political conscience and an indifference to principle, whether on the questions of Parliamentary reform or Protection. He was also annoyed by a strongly pro-Danish speech in the House by Disraeli in April 1848.

Neither the Queen nor Prince Albert welcomed the advent of Lord Derby's Protectionist government (February–December 1852) in which Disraeli served as Chancellor of the Exchequer as he was to again in 1858–59 and 1866–67. Experience of office gave him a feeling for Prince Albert which he described as being 'without exaggeration, one of affection'. By 1861 their relations had improved, but the Prince still nurtured strong mistrust.

Edward Geoffrey Stanley, fourteenth Earl of Derby (1799–1869)
Engraving by Henry Cousins after a painting by H. P. Briggs, 1842 (British Museum)

The Tory split of 1846 left the Protectionist backbenchers bereft of leadership and, after two years under Lord George Bentinck, they elected Lord Stanley as Party leader, but the dynamic guiding force in the Commons was Benjamin Disraeli.

Originally a follower of Canning, Stanley served in Earl Grey's 'Reform Bill Cabinet' as Colonial Secretary, introducing the bill for the abolition of slavery. He drifted back to the Tories, holding the same office under Peel, but resigned when Peel declared in favour of the complete and immediate abolition of the Corn Laws. In his finest speech in the House of Lords (25 May 1846) he insisted on the need for Protection as the mainstay of the landed interest and of the colonial system, the two pillars of empire. Disraeli in 1844 termed him, 'Rupert of debate, in his charge he is resistless, but when he returns from the pursuit he always finds his camp in the possession of the enemy.' He was a man of intense vitality rather than great intellect or philosophic statesmanship and devoted more time and money to sport than to politics.

He succeeded as Earl of Derby in 1851 and formed a government in 1852 and again in 1858–59, in each case with Disraeli as his right-hand man and Chancellor. The strength of the Conservative Party under their leadership lay in its compactness and discipline, despite its inability to secure a majority. These factors came to inspire the respect of Prince Albert who had earlier regarded Derby as immature and, with the Queen, detested the advent of a Protectionist government. Lord Derby made various advances to gain the support of Palmerston or at least an understanding with him to hold up the course of Parliamentary reform. Furthermore, the Prince found himself increasingly in sympathy with the Derby government over Italy. It left office in 1859 defeated but not discredited and with the satisfaction that the Conservative Party stood higher in popular esteem than at any time since 1846.

The Crimean War and Balmoral

George Hamilton Gordon, fourth Earl of Aberdeen (1784–1860)
Painting by John Partridge, 1847 (National Portrait Gallery)

Orphaned at the age of eleven, Lord Aberdeen became the ward of William Pitt, then wageing his titanic struggle against the French Republic. 'I was bred at the feet of Gamaliel and must always regard Mr. Pitt as the first of statesmen,' he said half a century later. He returned in 1803 from a European tour, which included Greece, an ardent Philhellene, and founded the Athenian Society. In 1812 he published *An Introduction containing an Historical View of the Rise and Progress of Architecture amongst the Greeks,* prefixed to a translation of *The Civil Architecture of Vitruvius,* and served as president of the Society of Antiquaries from 1812 to 1846.

Aberdeen was sent as Special Ambassador to Austria in 1813–14 which gave him an understanding of the problems of that state. During his tenures as Foreign Secretary under Wellington (1828–30) and Peel (1841–46) his policies contrasted by their quiet diplomacy with the more flamboyant ones of Palmerston, with whom he alternated at the Foreign Office. Aberdeen was on terms of friendship with Guizot, which facilitated the *entente cordiale* sealed by the exchange of royal visits with Louis Philippe, and these factors made him persona grata with Prince Albert. He was a faithful supporter of Peel and became the recognized leader of the Peelites after his chief's death.

Aberdeen considered in 1852 that all government must be progressive, 'Conservative progress if you please', and applied to himself the dictum of Pope, 'The Tories call me Whig, the Whigs a Tory'. On the fall of the Derby government he formed a coalition government of Peelites, Whigs and a Radical, united in supporting Free Trade and moderate progress, but the advent of the 'Eastern Crisis' and the drift into the Crimean War, due largely to his lack of firmness, showed up the defects of British military organization and he had to give place to Palmerston in January 1855.

William Ewart Gladstone (1809–1898)
Engraving by F. C. Lewis after a drawing by George Richmond, 1849 (British Museum)

Gladstone was a very devout High Anglican, educated at Eton and Oxford. He entered Parliament as a Tory in 1832 and received junior office under Peel, becoming his principal assistant in the work of reforming the tariff and finally serving as President of the Board of Trade. In the Conservative Party split he was one of the closest supporters of Peel, 'upon the whole the greatest man I ever knew'. Admiration for Peel and loyalty to his commercial and budgetary policies were to be his guiding light during the political flux of the ensuing years. This loyalty and his strong distrust of Disraeli's political character lay at the root of the two men's rivalry.

It was Gladstone's speech in December 1852 denouncing Disraeli's budget as dishonest, which largely determined its rejection and the fall of the Derby government.

104 The Crimean War and Balmoral

As Chancellor in the subsequent coalition government of Lord Aberdeen, Gladstone's budgets initiated a new financial era.

Prince Albert entertained a high esteem for Gladstone, 'For whatever his peculiar crotchets may be, he is a man of the strictest feelings of honour and the purest mind.' Gladstone admired the Prince's well-ordered life and untiring sense of duty. When the Prince died, the Queen seemed to think that of all her Ministers Gladstone had most entered into her sorrows. She thanked him in a 'letter of passionate desolation' for a panegyric on the Prince in 1862.

'The death of the Prince Consort was a greater personal calamity to Mr. Gladstone than he could then foresee... and it is impossible to doubt that if the Prince had survived at the Queen's right hand, certain jars might have been avoided that made many difficulties for the Minister in later times.' Few can disagree with John Morley's comment.

The Coalition Ministry of Lord Aberdeen, 1852–55
Pencil and wash drawing by Sir John Gilbert, 1854 (National Portrait Gallery)

In the 1852 elections the Tory government gained seats but not a majority, and so Disraeli's budget was rejected and the Derby ministry resigned. Despite Disraeli's prophetic closing words, 'This too, I know, that England does not love coalitions', only a coalition of Whigs and Peelites could have been assured of a majority with Radical support. Prince Albert too was doubtful of the efficacy or morality of a coalition government.

Aberdeen, as Prime Minister, aimed at forming 'a liberal Conservative government in the sense of that of Sir Robert Peel' and, in Palmerston's words, it included 'almost all the men of talent and experience in the House of Commons except Disraeli'. In that sense it contrasted favourably with its predecessor. Offices were divided fairly equally between the Whigs and Radicals, who controlled more seats in the House, and the Peelites, who provided the greater wealth of ability. On the whole the cabinet worked in greater harmony than many of its members anticipated, and it marked the first step towards the ultimate fusion of Peelites, Whigs and Radicals into Liberals in 1859.

Unfortunately the Aberdeen government was faced with the 'Eastern Crisis' caused by Russian threats to the Turkish empire. Lord Aberdeen was considered too weak and appeasing and as a result, in alliance with France, Britain found herself at war in March 1854. This painting shows the cabinet adopting in June 1854 Palmerston's plan for striking at Russia in the Crimea and taking Sebastopol. The Army was unprepared, there was gross mismanagement resulting in great suffering by the troops, and when the House of Commons approved Roebuck's motion for a committee of inquiry into the conduct of the war, the government was forced to resign in January 1855. The members depicted are, left to right: Sir Charles Wood (W), President of the Board of Control; Sir James Graham (P), First Lord of the Admiralty; Sir William Molesworth (Radical), First Commissioner of Works; W. E. Gladstone (P), Chancellor of the Exchequer; Duke of Argyll (P), Lord Privy Seal; Lord Clarendon (W), Foreign Secretary; Marquess of Lansdowne (W), Cabinet Minister without office; Lord John Russell (W), Leader of the House of Commons; Earl Granville (W), Lord President of the Council; Earl of Aberdeen (P), Prime Minister; Lord Cranworth (W), Lord Chancellor; Viscount Palmerston (W), Home Secretary; Sir George Grey (W), Secretary for Colonies; Sidney Herbert (P), Secretary at War; Duke of Newcastle (P), Secretary for War.

[W: Whig; P: Peelite.]

The Crimean War and Balmoral

106 *The Crimean War and Balmoral*

(*opposite top*)
Back view of the Old House at Balmoral, looking towards the River Dee
Watercolour by James Giles, 1849 (Royal Collection)

In a letter to the Duchess of Coburg from Balmoral in September 1848, Prince Albert wrote, 'We have withdrawn for a short time into a complete mountain solitude, where one rarely sees a human face, where the snow already covers the mountain tops, and the wild deer come creeping round the house... This place belonged to poor Sir Robert Gordon, Lord Aberdeen's brother.'

Though the Gordons were the original owners of Balmoral, when Sir Robert acquired the lease from the Fife trustees, he became the first member of his family to live in the castle for over one hundred and seventy years. He died suddenly on 8 October 1847. A very wet tour round the west coast of Scotland in 1847 did nothing to diminish the Queen's and Prince Albert's affection for the Highlands, nor abate their desire to find a residence there. Learning that the climate of Deeside was not only sunnier, but drier, and impressed by sketches of the house and estate by the Aberdeen artist, James Giles, they accepted Lord Aberdeen's suggestion that they should take over the lease of Balmoral forthwith. They saw the castle for the first time in 1848.

(*opposite bottom*)
Crathie Kirk, Deeside, 1849
Watercolour by W. H. Fisk (Royal Collection)

Since the time of Queen Victoria, Crathie Kirk has been the regular place of worship of the Royal Family when at Balmoral. Standing on a grassy platform above the River Dee, it was built in 1804 to replace a fifteenth-century church and was itself replaced in 1895. John Brown, the Queen and Prince's faithful attendant, was buried in the kirkyard in 1883.

Prince Albert liked the Scots Presbyterian form of worship, finding it more akin to German Lutheranism than was the Church of England. With the years the Queen came increasingly to appreciate the Scots service. From 1872 on she took communion every autumn at Crathie. Lord Aberdeen much regretted the Royal Family's having thrown off the English church altogether on their visits to Scotland. At first he thought it right that they should go to kirk, but when they became residents he lamented that they did not bring their chaplain with them. When Gladstone was Minister-in-Attendance in autumn 1863 he attended an Episcopal service in the Free Kirk schoolroom at Ballater. 'I believe this is about the first expedition ever made from Balmoral to an Episcopal service... There was *no* chaplain here today, and so no dining room service, which for many I fear means no service at all,' he wrote (4 October 1863).

Drawing Room at Balmoral, September 1857
Watercolour by J. Roberts (Royal Collection)

'The Queen's apartments above look towards Invercauld... The general woodwork is lightcoloured, maple and birch chiefly, with locks and hinges, etc. silvered, and the effect is very good... Chandeliers of Parian; Highlanders, beautifully designed figures, holding the light and which are placed in appropriate trophies—table ornaments in the same style, and loads of curiously devised and tasteful, as well as elaborately executed articles... The carpets are Royal Stuart tartan and green Hunting Stuart, the curtains, the former lined with red, the same dress Stuart and a few chintz with a thistle pattern, the chairs and sofas in the Drawing Room are 'dress Stuart' poplin. All highly characteristic and appropriate, but not all equally flatteux to the eye.' Thus did Lady Augusta Stanley, a favourite lady-in-waiting to the Queen, describe the apartments into which the Royal Family moved on 7 September 1855.

The Crimean War and Balmoral

Balmoral, with the New and Old House, from the opposite side of the Dee, October 1855
Anonymous watercolour (Royal Collection)

Immediately after 1848 Queen Victoria and Prince Albert lost no time in negotiating the purchase of what the Queen described as the 'pretty little castle in the old Scottish style'. John Smith, an Aberdeen architect, who had made the alterations to Balmoral for Sir Robert Gordon, was summoned by Prince Albert to discuss further additions, and the possibility of building a new house. However, the legal transactions were prolonged, and it was only in 1852 that Prince Albert finally acquired Balmoral. John Smith had now been succeeded by his son William, and he, together with the Prince, drew up plans for a house sited one hundred yards from the old castle and with much finer views up the river.

The foundation stone of the new house, praised later by Queen Victoria as 'my dear Albert's *own* creation, own building, own laying-out, as at *Osborne*', was laid in September 1853. By 1855 the new Balmoral was sufficiently completed to allow the Queen and Prince to reside in the new building, the gentlemen-in-waiting and the servants still being housed in the old castle. By 1856, however, to the possible regret of Lord Aberdeen, all traces of the original home of the Gordons had been swept away.

The Crimean War and Balmoral 109

Gillies' or Servants' Ball, Balmoral, 1859
Watercolour attributed to Egon Lundgren (Royal Collection)

Writing to the Princess Royal in September 1859, the Prince Consort concluded, 'Yesterday we had the Gillies' Ball, at which Arthur [later Duke of Connaught] distinguished himself, and was greatly applauded in the Highland reels; next to Jemie Gow he was the "favourite in the room".'

Queen Victoria first watched a sword dance at Dunkeld, during her visit to Scotland in 1842. 'Two swords are crossed and laid upon the ground, and the dancer has to dance across them without touching them.'

Prince Albert in Highland Dress
Lithograph by J. A. Vinter after a painting by Kenneth Macleay (British Museum)

(*opposite*)
The Prince of Wales and Prince Alfred
Lithograph by Léon Noel after a painting by Franz Xaver Winterhalter, 1849 (British Museum)

110 *The Crimean War and Balmoral*

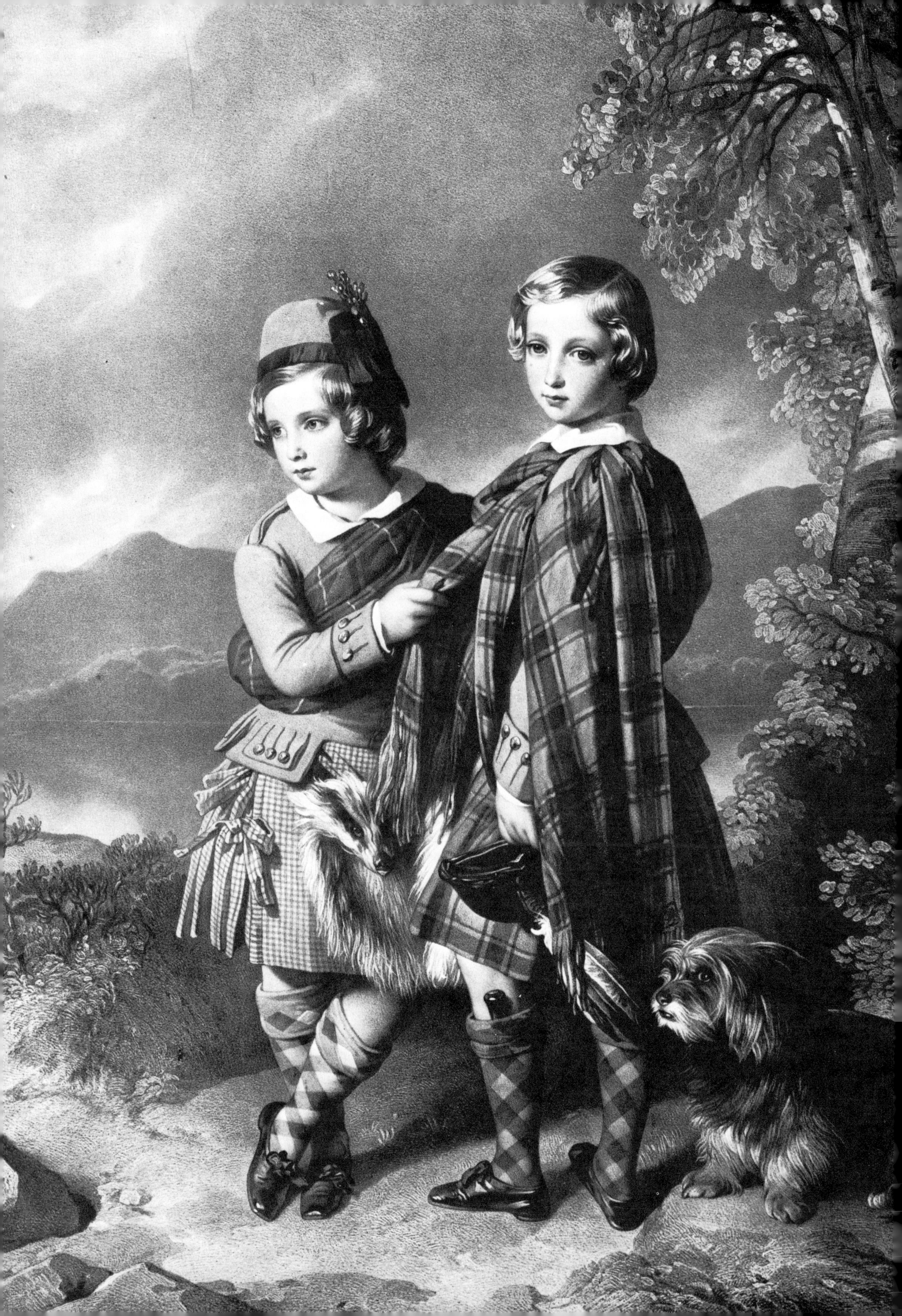

The Princess Royal, Princess Frederick William of Prussia, with Prince William of Prussia, later William II, German Emperor
Engraving by R. J. Lane from a photograph, May 1859 (British Museum)

On 30 January 1859 the Prince Consort wrote to Augusta, Princess of Prussia, 'I must write to join with you in thanks to God for the great blessing that has been vouchsafed to us.' No baby was more ardently desired or welcomed by its grandparents than William, the first child of Prince Frederick William of Prussia and the Princess Royal. He seemed to be the embodiment of all Prince Albert's ideals of a Liberal German Empire led by Prussia in close alliance with Great Britain, the future German Kaiser, grandson of the Queen of England and of the Prince, later King, of Prussia.

The influence of his Prussian grandfather and of Bismarck was deliberately to alienate him over the years from his mother and her country. So the boy who seemed the seal of Albert's work and hopes was to turn into the doom of Victoria's empire, unleashing two World Wars and finally shattering that German unity to which his father and grandfather had devoted their lives.

The Prussian Marriage: Prince Albert's German Dream

After his engagement to the Queen, Prince Albert wrote to his grandmother, the Duchess of Gotha (28 November 1839), 'I shall never cease to be a true German, Coburger and Gothaner', and he remained true to his word. Lord Malmesbury, vindicating the Prince against the absurd canards current on the eve of the Crimean War, concluded 'his heart is naturally German'.

Prince Albert saw no contradiction between loyalty to his native and to his adopted country. Both, the two leading Protestant nations in Europe, had so much in common and so much to give each other. Germany had given England the Protestant faith with its vernacular liturgy and a Royal House to defend it. England showed the Germans how constitutional government was the best safeguard of national unity, and no nation had shown more appreciation than the Germans for Shakespeare, an acknowledged fountainhead of that literary efflorescence which made the Germans conscious of their cultural unity and anxious to implement it politically. Together they would counterbalance the pressures of Russian despotism and of a restless Bonapartist France, with its 'Party of Movement'.

Bonn infused Albert with a passion for German unity under the leadership of Prussia, the largest purely German and predominantly Protestant state. His mentor on the Italian journey, Stockmar, joined to this ideal which he shared, a vocation to help establish a unity of purpose between Germany and England on which the peace and progress of Europe depended. The achievement of these twin ideals became the purpose of Albert's life as the husband to England's Queen, and in this pursuit their children, especially the two eldest, were to have key rôles. The establishment of an Anglo-Prussian Bishopric of Jerusalem was a foretaste. In Bunsen, the Prussian Minister who negotiated it, Prince Albert found a kindred spirit. Together they brought Friedrich List, the economist and protagonist of German economic unity through railways and tariff protection, into contact with Sir Robert Peel. List, one of the few Germans who observed and understood Great Britain and her economy, was present in the House of Commons gallery when the vote in favour of the abolition of the Corn Laws took place. He endeavoured to enlist Peel's support for his proposals for a close Anglo-German alliance, albeit combined with German tariff protection, the latter proposal vitiating the former in Peel's view.

Frederick William IV of Prussia was specially invited to England in 1842 to stand godfather to the heir, the Prince of Wales, while four years later, when Augusta, Princess of Prussia, visited Windsor and forged her close friendship with the Queen, the idea took shape of a marriage between her son, Prince Frederick William, the heir presumptive, after his father, to the Prussian crown, and the precocious Princess Royal.

In 1851 Prince Frederick William visited England with his parents and a relationship of admiring disciple and zealous tutor was established between him and the Queen's consort. Prince Albert wrote in the young man's autograph book, 'May Prussia be merged in Germany and not Germany in Prussia'. The key to Albert's dream for Germany was not that it should become a greater Prussia, but rather that Prussia's Royal House should assume the headship of a new Liberal German Empire. The failure to realize such a hope for nearly a century, and then without the Hohenzollerns, was to cost both Albert's countries dear and to cloud his memory enduringly in Victoria's realm. She, like her subjects, failed to grasp sufficiently this imperative distinction made by her consort, and the fatal misinterpretation could not be set right because the tomb had closed over Albert.

The Princess Royal became engaged to Frederick

William at Balmoral, where the bonfires were celebrating the fall of Sebastopol in September 1855. If Prince Albert and the Queen and Princess Augusta were delighted, the reactionary pro-Russian party in Berlin were incensed and *The Times* fumed. The young couple embarked in January 1858 on a marriage which was completely happy personally, but doomed to tragedy politically. During the months before her marriage the Princess translated, at her father's behest, J. G. Droysen's pamphlet on the German policy of Karl August, Duke of Weimar, Princess Augusta's grandfather. Albert sent it to Lord Clarendon, the Foreign Secretary, who replied, 'In reading Droysen, I felt that the motto of Prussia should be "Semper eadem", and in thinking of his translator, I felt that she is destined to change that motto into the "Vigilando ascendimus" of Weimar.'

Alas, the Princess soon found herself as much misconstrued in Berlin as ever her father had been in England. It was a supreme tragic irony that she, who had willingly become the adoring vehicle for her German father's idealistic aims for his native country, should be denounced there as 'the Englishwoman', while he himself remained 'the Queen's German husband' in England. She felt the same homesickness that he had and so he wrote to her (24 March 1858), 'It is a painful yearning, which may exist quite independently of, and simultaneously with complete contentment and complete happiness.'

Prince Albert appreciated her difficulties when he wrote to her after the birth of her fateful first-born (9 February 1859), 'It was a year from yesterday that you went to Berlin, and nineteen years since I came to London. My nineteen years have not gone much slower to me than your one has to you. What will it look like after the next nineteen years?' On 13 September of the same year he wrote again, 'I am for Prussia's hegemony; still *Germany* is for me first in importance, Prussia as Prussia second. Prussia will become the chief if she stand at the head of Germany; if she merely seek to drag Germany down to herself, she will not herself ascend.' Prussia's reactionaries regarded Albert as an interloper because he was not a Prussian and took the larger German view.

Prince Albert died in December 1861, and Bismarck was called to power in Prussia by William I in September 1862 in open defiance of the Prussian Parliament. He set out on his policy of unifying Germany by the 'Blood and Iron' of foreign wars. Prince Albert realized by the last year of his life that the Liberal 'New Era' initiated by the Prince of Prussia as regent had been sacrificed to the exigencies of Roon and the generals. He wrote to King Leopold (4 July 1861), 'There exists in Prussia a great Junker and bureaucrats' party which comes together in the Army and particularly in the Guards, which is determined not to allow the constitution and constitutional government to develop, and which for this purpose does not shrink from cunning, fraud and violence for the provocation of a revolution or of a coup d'état and ... the King himself belongs to this party by sympathy and by tradition.' This party was to dominate the German Reich, Imperial and Republican, and finally bring Hitler to power in its own *Götterdämmerung*. Prince Albert warned his son-in-law, the Crown Prince, that 'an *external* war for the elimination of *internal* dissension and evils is always a morally unjustified undertaking' (1 May 1861).

Those wars of Bismarck were to disrupt Albert's and Victoria's own family. The Prince had agreed that the only princess suitable for the Prince of Wales was Alexandra, daughter of Prince Christian, heir to the throne of Denmark with Schleswig-Holstein. This nearly caused a rupture with his brother Ernest, patron of the Liberal National Verein because German opinion supported the claim to Schleswig-Holstein, with its predominantly German population, of Prince Frederick of Augustenburg, who was married to Princess Feodora's daughter. Albert denounced to King Leopold the hypocrisy of the Prussian government 'which makes an immoral "convenience" of the Holstein question, lays stress in Denmark upon the maintenance of the rights of the Estates [of Holstein] to control their own Budget, and at home raises money for the augmentation of the Army without the knowledge of the Chambers, and in the face of all its promises to them, and which in its heart will not listen to a word on the subject of popular rights' (3 May 1861).

In the event Bismarck was to seize the duchies from Denmark in 1864 and then 'discover' that King Christian, who had ceded them under force of arms to Prussia and Austria, had a better claim than Prince Frederick after all. So, having defeated Austria in 1866, Prussia retained them. In the process Palmerston, Prime Minister again since 1859, proved completely ineffective and the Queen supported the German cause 'because the Prince would have wished it'. Palmerston and Russell, the last of the Whigs, were to be completely outwitted by the greatest of the Junkers. The Princess Royal, Crown Princess of Prussia, applauded Prussia's victories until hard experience made her realize the price she and her husband had to pay for Bismarck's success and the betrayal of her father's ideals.

The formation of Palmerston's government in 1859 also marked the end of that period of flux initiated by Peel's abolition of the Corn Laws. Whigs, Peelites and Radicals became fused in one Liberal Party, and as Palmerston and Russell faded into impotence and obscurity, Gladstone emerged as its natural leader against Disraeli, the dominant figure on the Conservative side.

Frederick William IV, King of Prussia (1795–1861)
Anonymous engraving after a portrait (British Museum)

'The Romantic on the Throne', Frederick William IV felt called to mediate between the extremes of Catholicism and revolution. To this end he sought a close relationship with Protestant Britain, an idea most congenial to Prince Albert. After his accession in 1840 he therefore sent Bunsen in 1841 to negotiate the foundation of the joint Anglo-Prussian Bishopric of Jerusalem. This was to be a manifestation of Protestant presence in the Holy Land in face of the Turkish authorities and of Catholic and Orthodox disputes there.

In January 1842 he was invited to England by the Queen and Prince Albert on Stockmar's initiative, to be godfather to the Prince of Wales. This was generally approved by British opinion. 'Well may we exclaim, what next,' purred Bunsen, when the Queen issued the invitation through him. Russia, Austria and France sought to dissuade the King from attending the christening, while the court party at Berlin feared that with Bunsen and the Archbishop of Canterbury he might pursue his favourite idea of Anglicanizing the Prussian Church, wherein his father had forcibly fused Lutherans and Calvinists. The Queen found him 'entertaining, agreeable and witty' and a firm friendship and frequent correspondence resulted. At Frederick William's request Queen Victoria arranged for him to meet the prison reformer, Elizabeth Fry. In the 1848 revolution he played a vacillating part and subsequently relied on reactionary Ministers. In 1858 he lost his reason, and his brother, who was also his heir, acted as regent.

The Prussian Marriage 115

Christian Josias von Bunsen (1791–1860)
Engraving by H. Robinson after a drawing by G. Richmond (British Museum)

After serving under Niebuhr in the Prussian legation in Rome, Bunsen became Minister there from 1827 to 1838, founding the Prussian Archaeological Institute. While there he married Frances Waddington of Llanover and also won the favour of the Crown Prince of Prussia, after 1840 Frederick William IV, by his liturgical plans.

He was therefore sent to London in 1841 to negotiate the new King's pet idea of a joint Anglican-Lutheran Bishopric of Jerusalem. He found a starting point in the English Mission to the Jews. An English bishopric was founded by Act of Parliament and endowed half by the King of Prussia and half by individual English subscribers. German missions and congregations were to enjoy its protection. It was welcomed by the Archbishop of Canterbury and the Evangelicals, but opposed by the Tractarians and provided the initial impetus which ultimately in October 1845 led Newman to join the Church of Rome. The first incumbent of the bishopric was Professor Michael Solomon Alexander of King's College, London, a Prussian Jew of the Anglican persuasion.

This success led to Bunsen's appointment as Prussian Minister in London where he was welcomed by the Queen and Prince Albert. He installed the legation in Carlton House Terrace, where it remained for a century. Convinced of Prussia's right to lead Germany, Bunsen felt his own rôle to be that of a mediator between her and Britain. He became very friendly with Prince Albert, maintaining a regular, frank correspondence. There was a mutual attraction with Peel, the only British statesman with whom he could discuss German affairs openly in 1848–49; the Tories were hostile, the Whigs apathetic. Peel on his deathbed was reported to have asked three times for Bunsen. He was also a close friend of Gladstone.

Caroline Fox found in him, 'Far more real beauty than I expected, exquisite chiselling about the mouth and chin, large grey eyes, a certain vagueness and dreaminess, but also a general decision of character in the expression of the face and a fine glow of genial feeling over all.'

His failure to win British support over Schleswig-Holstein in 1848–50 and his over-zealous but ineffectual attempts to bring Prussia on to the British side in the Crimean War led to his retirement in 1854.

(*opposite*)
William I, King of Prussia, later German Emperor (1797–1888)
Lithograph by Georg Engelbach after a painting by Franz Xaver Winterhalter (British Museum)

The younger brother of King Frederick William IV, the Prince of Prussia was essentially a soldier in the Prussian tradition. The obduracy of the 'Cartridge Prince' in face of the March 1848 revolution in Berlin forced him to flee to London at the end of the month. Here he was warmly welcomed by Prince Albert, who had been much attracted by his frank and open soldierly manner when they met during the Queen's visit to Germany in 1845. In 1848 Albert was much impressed by his visitor's courage and lack of vindictiveness in face of adversity and endeavoured, as he thought with success, to win him over to support a constitutional solution under the crown to Prussia's difficulties as a means to German unification. 'Men like him Germany cannot do without now and it would be sad if a stigma remained on the heir to the Prussian throne,' Prince Albert wrote to King Leopold (28 March 1848). Such constitutionalism was in line with the views of Prince William's wife Augusta of Saxe-Weimar, Princess of Prussia, who gained temporarily in influence over him and welcomed the support of the Queen and Prince Albert. Prince William returned to Prussia at the end of May. With their son and daughter, they visited London for the opening of the Great Exhibition and they were among the leaders of the pro-western party in Prussia during the Crimean War. There was also a steady correspondence with the Queen and Prince Albert.

In 1858 Prince William became regent for his mentally incapacitated brother and replaced the reactionary government by one more favourable to the cause of German unity. The regent was, however, primarily a soldier and so, with the new War Minister Albrecht von Roon, he insisted on longer military service and other measures which were eventually to give a Prussian militarist impress to German society, but which at the time aroused strong opposition among the overwhelming Liberal majority in Prussia's Parliament.

In 1861 he succeeded his brother and crowned himself at Königsberg with unsurpassed splendour. In a ceremony which aroused Prince Albert's contempt, he claimed, 'I am the first King to mount the throne since it has been supported by modern institutions, but I do not forget that the Crown has come to me from God alone and that I have received it at His hands.' Accordingly in September 1862 he entrusted the government to Otto von Bismarck who was determined to overcome the opposition of the Prussian Parliament and to unify Germany by 'Blood and Iron' with the unswerving support of his King. It marked the final failure of Prince Albert's endeavours in that sphere.

116 The Prussian Marriage

The Prussian Marriage 117

Augusta, Queen of Prussia, later German Empress (1811–1890)
Lithograph by G. Feckert after a painting by Franz Xaver Winterhalter (British Museum)

The granddaughter of Karl August, Duke of Saxe-Weimar, who had sought a reform of the old Holy Roman Empire under Prussian leadership before the revolutionary and Napoleonic waves swept over Germany, Augusta was enduringly impressed by her youthful acquaintance with Goethe. This encouraged her taste for literature, music and the fine arts in which she showed considerable skill. In the atmosphere of Goethe's Weimar she had conceived strong sympathies for the west and its Liberalism and an antipathy to Russia despite the fact that her mother was a Russian grand duchess. In 1829 she contracted a marriage with Prince William of Prussia, her intellectual inferior, which was never very harmonious. His heart had been lost to the Polish Princess Elise Radziwill, who was not *ebenbürtig*, while Augusta felt herself to represent the German Athens in a Prussian Sparta.

She first met Queen Victoria on the Rhine in 1845 and visited Windsor in 1846. The

118 The Prussian Marriage

Queen found her 'so clever, so amiable, so well-informed and so good, she seems to have some enemies, for there are whispers of her being *false*; but from all that I have seen of her... I *cannot* and will not believe it. Her position is a very difficult one; she is too enlightened and liberal for the Prussian Court not to have enemies; but *I believe* that she is a friend to us and our family, and I do believe that *I* have a friend in her, who may be most useful to us' (letter to King Leopold, 29 September 1846).

Augusta's western sympathies brought her into sharp conflict during the Crimean War with the reactionary pro-Russian party in Prussia, including Bismarck. This was exacerbated by her close friendship with Queen Victoria and Prince Albert. Countess Bernstoff wrote in 1855, 'Queen Victoria is the only person who has any influence with the Princess being quite an oracle to her.' She welcomed the marriage of her adored only son to the Princess Royal. Yet though their political sympathies were similar and she was such a close friend of the Princess's parents, there were always strains if not open enmity in her personal relationship with her daughter-in-law.

The Princess Royal and Prince Frederick William of Prussia, later Frederick III, King of Prussia and German Emperor (1831–1888)
Lithograph by Carl Suessnapp, 1858 (British Museum)

Prince Frederick William, 'Fritz', first visited England with his parents in 1851 for the opening of the Great Exhibition. A shy young man, he was fascinated by the self-confidence of the ten-year-old Princess Royal and filled with devoted admiration for her father with his clear ideals for a liberal Germany. Fritz, the great-grandson of Karl August of Weimar, shared his mother's similar aims. Prince Albert saw in her and her son a means by which he too could contribute materially to the consummation of his life's great dream of a united liberal Germany.

In September 1855 Fritz came to Balmoral and the mutual attraction with Vicky reached new dimensions. It was agreed by the Queen and Prince Albert that they might marry in due course after her confirmation. Meanwhile Prince Albert supervised the education of his daughter for her new rôle and wrote memoranda of instruction for his future son-in-law.

On 25 January 1858 they were married in the Chapel Royal at St. James's Palace. The Princess had a triumphal reception in Berlin. 'The enthusiasm and interest shown are beyond everything. Never was a Princess in this country received as she is,' wrote Princess Feodora to the Queen (17 February 1858). Ernst Moritz Arndt, the veteran patriotic poet of the War of Liberation against Napoleon, who had enthused Albert in Bonn, cried out 'Victoria in Berlin, may an English spirit blow through us!' All this gave intense happiness to the Prince Consort. But the reactionary Junker element at court, who looked to Russia, deplored her arrival, seeing in the 'English Marriage' an infection of absolutist Prussia with libertarian ideas propagated by the bride's parents and mother-in-law. Fritz, whose education had been impaired in its Prussian purity by the influence of his Weimar mother, was now in their view to be intellectually dwarfed and subjugated by his English wife. Behind her stood Prince Albert who wrote to his brother (12 July 1861), 'I am very satisfied with Fritz. It is not possible to develop more steadily and well from a political point of view than he has done lately, or rather, since his marriage.' Such were the roots of the forces which for thirty years were to attack and undermine this happy young couple, because they represented the ideals of Prince Albert of Coburg, the ideals of another Germany.

Medal
Issued to Commemorate the Marriage, 25 January 1858, of Prince Frederick William of Prussia to the Princess Royal (British Museum)

The Prussian Marriage 119

Alexandra of Denmark, Princess of Wales, later Queen of England (1844–1926)
Painting by Richard Lauchert (Royal Collection)

Princess Alexandra was the eldest daughter of Prince Christian of Glücksburg, whom the Treaty of London in 1850 had recognized as heir to the Danish crown and to Schleswig-Holstein, while German opinion wanted the latter duchies to go to Prince Frederick of Augustenburg. It was clear to Queen Victoria and Prince Albert that the princess who might hope to hold the affections of the Prince of Wales must have 'good looks, health, education, character, intellect and a good disposition', also a certain determination. The search for such a paragon was confided in 1859 to their daughter 'Vicky'. Her lady-in-waiting, Walburga Lady Paget, first interested Prince Albert in Princess Alexandra as a prospective daughter-in-law at dinner at Windsor in October 1860. When he saw her photograph he exclaimed 'I would marry her at once', while the Queen found it lovely but added in view of the Schleswig-Holstein complications, 'what a pity she is who she is!'

The Prince of Wales was immediately attracted when he met Alexandra 'accidentally' in Speyer Cathedral. Then he hesitated, but his father urged him not to lose 'positive and present advantages for the hope of future chances which may never occur' (7 October 1861). The Prince Consort's death upset the rhythm of romance, but in September 1862 the Queen met Princess Alexandra and her parents at Laeken and with her approval the Prince proposed there and was accepted. 'How he [Prince Albert] would have doted on her and loved her!' was the Queen's comment. From her there could be no higher praise for the beautiful girl who was so soon to win the hearts of all England.

> For Saxon or Dane or Norman we,
> Teuton or Celt, or whatever we be,
> We are each all Dane in our welcome of thee,
>   Alexandra!

sang the Poet Laureate, Tennyson.

German nationalist opinion considered that Prince Albert had betrayed the cause he had so long supported by approving the Danish match. Slanderous reports concerning the morality of Princess Alexandra's mother were set in motion by, among others, Olympia von Usedom, wife of Prussia's Liberal representative at Frankfurt. The Princess Royal went to great pains to ascertain their complete falseness for Queen Victoria. There was nearly a breach

120 *The Prussian Marriage*

with Ernest, Duke of Coburg, who endeavoured in his fury to wreck the project. This earned him an extremely stern letter of rebuke from the Prince Consort for his breach of confidence (21 July 1861). Stockmar questioned disapprovingly whether Alexandra had besides youth and beauty, 'the important moral powers that we need' to compensate for those wanting in the Prince of Wales. The marriage took place on 10 March 1863 at St. George's Chapel, Windsor.

Albert Edward, Prince of Wales, later Edward VII, King of England (1841–1910)
Miniature by D. Mossman, 1861 (Royal Collection)

The Prince of Wales was born in November 1841 and the Queen's pregnancy therefore coincided with the difficulties of the transition from Melbourne to Peel and the separation shortly after from Lehzen. From the first he was overshadowed by his brilliantly precocious older sister, the Princess Royal, who responded completely to all Prince Albert's hopes and to his theories of education. The Prince of Wales, 'Bertie', was less responsive, and this was a root cause of misunderstanding with his father and therefore beyond the latter's grave with his mother.

The Prince of Wales inherited many of the Hanoverian traits of his mother's family, but also his great-uncle Leopold's ability to mix easily with people. His participation in his parents' visit to Paris in 1855 gave him a lasting affection for France expressed in his words to Napoleon III, 'I wish I were your son'.

In 1860 he made an official visit to Canada, following in the footsteps of his grandfather, the Duke of Kent. It was an enthusiastic success and proved his diplomatic abilities. He extended his visit to the United States, on an unofficial basis, the first member of the Royal Family to visit them since the War of Independence. With President James Buchanan he visited the tomb of George Washington, planting a tree to bury the last faint trace of discord, as *The Times* correspondent noted.

In 1861 Prince Albert purchased Sandringham for his son out of funds accumulated for the purpose. This was to become the family home for him and Princess Alexandra of Denmark, the wife approved for him by his parents, and for their children. The Princess Royal wrote to the Queen (13 February 1862), 'Marry early Bertie must; I am more convinced of that every day; he has not resisted small temptations, only launch him alone in the London Society and you will see what becomes of him.'

Prince William of Prussia, later William II, German Emperor (1859–1940)
Miniature by Anton Hähnisch, 1860 (Royal Collection)

On the first birthday of Prince William, here depicted with a rattle and a 'Hans Wurst' doll, Prince Albert wrote to his fellow grandfather, the Prince of Prussia, 'May God prosper the dear little one for the welfare of his country and the joy of us all.'

In September 1860 the Queen and Prince Albert made their last visit together to Coburg where for the first time they saw their first grandchild. 'Our darling grandchild was brought. Such a little love!. . . He is a fine fat child. . . with a very dear face, like Vicky and Fritz. . . We felt so happy to see him at last,' rejoiced the Queen, and again, 'Dear little William. . . he is such a darling, so intelligent.' Prince Albert wrote in similar vein to the Duchess of Kent.

The Prussian Marriage 121

Victoria, Duchess of Kent (1786–1861)
Painting by Franz Xaver Winterhalter
(National Portrait Gallery)

When Prince Albert became engaged to the Queen, her mother's influence was at its nadir. Lehzen, Melbourne and the Prince's brother were the first to be informed, then King Leopold and Stockmar. 'What grieves me is that my Aunt is not to know of it,' Albert wrote to Stockmar.

However, from the time of the Queen's marriage the Duchess's position and her relationship with her daughter began to improve. She owed this largely to Prince Albert to whom she was not merely mother-in-law but also aunt. He liked motherly women and the Duchess was the only person at court who could talk to him of his precious past at Coburg, which she revisited in 1841 for the first time since her second marriage. He found an obstacle in his domestic life in Lehzen, the person who had given Victoria support against her mother and Conroy and had emotionally displaced that mother. With the dismissal of Lehzen in 1842 Albert reigned supreme in the household, while the Duchess, already godmother to the Princess Royal in 1840, entered upon her rôle as grandmother. She was present at Coburg in 1845 to welcome the Queen to her own and Albert's home. She shared in the Scottish holidays at Blair Atholl and Balmoral.

The Duchess of Kent died on 16 March 1861, and the Queen, overwhelmed with distress, found in her mother's effects letters witnessing to the love and affection between her parents. 'I hardly knew it was *to that extent*. Then her love for *me*—it is *too* touching. . . Oh! I am so wretched to think *how for a time, two people* most wickedly estranged us!. . . I *dare not* think of it—it drives me *wild* now! But thank God! That is all passed *long, long* ago, and she had forgotten it. . . And all that was brought about by my good angel, dearest Albert, whom *she* adored, and in whom she had such unbounded confidence' (9 April 1861).

(*below*)
The Royal Family at Osborne, 1857
Photograph by Caldesi and Montecchi, published by Colnaghi and Co., 1858
(British Museum)

From left to right stand (back row): Prince Alfred, the Prince Consort, Princess Helena, Princess Alice, the Princess Royal, Princess Louise, the Prince of Wales; (front row): Prince Arthur, Queen Victoria holding Princess Beatrice, Prince Leopold.

122 The Prussian Marriage

Medal
Issued to Commemorate the Opening of the Victoria Bridge, Montreal, by the Prince of Wales, 1860 (British Museum)

Proposing a toast to the Prince of Wales and the rest of the Royal Family at a dinner of Trinity House on 23 June 1860, Prince Albert remarked, 'It will be a curious co-incidence, that nearly at the same time—a few weeks hence—though almost at the opposite poles, the Prince of Wales will inaugurate, in the Queen's name, that stupendous work, the great bridge over the St. Lawrence in Canada, while Prince Alfred will lay the foundation stone of the breakwater for the harbour of Cape Town.'

The Prussian Marriage 123

In Memory of Prince Albert
A tazza of glazed earthenware, designed by John Leighton, and carried out by W. T. Copeland, 1863. The engraver was C. H. Jeens. (National Portrait Gallery, on loan from Victoria and Albert Museum)

Among the various offices commemorated is that of the Prince's Chancellorship of Cambridge University to which he was elected by a very narrow majority in 1847.

The Tragic Dénouement: 1861

The year 1861 was to terminate in tragedy for Prince Albert, but the dénouement was hardly sudden. Events seemed to lead up to it. It was becoming increasingly apparent to him that the 'New Era' in Prussia on which he had set his hopes, was being undermined by the militarist policy of the new King William I who succeeded in January and crowned himself with unsurpassed splendour at Königsberg in October, insisting on his divine right. Prince Albert regarded it as a pantomime, but recognized that the friend in whom he had put his trust for Germany's future had betrayed it and was harking back to the absolutist past. Even his daughter seemed momentarily dazzled.

Meanwhile that daughter's position in Prussia was being eroded by the steady attacks on everything German in the British press led by *The Times*. Life in the unhealthy Prussian palaces led her to develop bronchitis and Dr. Wegner, so largely responsible for the bungling in her first pregnancy, wrote to Queen Victoria about double pneumonia, suggesting she might lose her daughter. Prince Albert's own personal physician had been killed in a railway accident in January. 'He is an incalculable loss,' was the record in his diary.

On 16 March the Duchess of Kent died. The Queen was so overwhelmed with grief that Lord Clarendon even feared her mind might become unhinged. Her own half-sister Feodora could not console her. Victoria wrote to King Leopold, '*She* is gone. That *precious dearly beloved tender Mother*—whom I never was parted from but for a few months—without whom *I* can't *imagine life*—has been taken from us . . . Dearest Albert is dreadfully overcome—and well he may be, for *she* adored him' (16 March 1861). Prince Albert not only lost a beloved aunt, but also came in the front line of the Queen's hysterical outbursts of grief, tinged no doubt with a certain remorse. He had had a foretaste in 1844 when his father died and in 1850 when Queen Louise of the Belgians died. Prince Albert was the Duchess's sole executor, her comptroller had died a fortnight before and the estate was highly complicated and almost insolvent.

In November tragedy struck again. Prince Albert's cousin, Ferdinand of Coburg, had married Maria II, Queen of Portugal and Albert hoped that a new dynasty of Coburg-Braganças might bring that country into the new Liberal comity of western Europe and emulate the Aviz-Lancasters of Portugal's heroic age. Now the young King Pedro V, who had succeeded his mother in 1853, and one of his brothers died of typhoid fever, to be followed by a third brother just after Christmas. The Prince Consort had loved the young King 'like a son', as Queen Victoria said, and pinned great hopes on him for Portugal's future. 'He was so attached to my beloved Albert'. The Prince wrote of his bereavement to Stockmar and added, 'I am fearfully in want of a true friend and counsellor, and that *you* are the friend and counsellor I want, you will readily understand' (14 November 1861). But Stockmar was old and failing and never returned to England after 1857 despite entreaties from the Prince, who lamented to Lord Clarendon that good men are 'being cut off in the midst of their usefulness, while bad ones are left to do harm with apparent impunity'.

As the old generation was passing away and the young increased and grew up, so it brought problems with it. The Prince of Wales had returned to Cambridge University after spending a part of his vacation with the army at the Curragh. While there he had had an affair with an actress, Nellie Clifden. Prince Albert was already a sick man when he went to Cambridge to see his errant but contrite son on 25 November. He feared that news of the affair might upset the plans for an engagement to Princess Alexandra. His own father's affair with Madame Panam had ruined the prospect of marriage to a Russian grand duchess. Moreover at the back of the Prince Consort's mind there must always have lurked the memories of the Queen's uncles and the ever present worries about his own brother's misdemeanours and consequent financial exigencies. He could recall the pure hedonism of Charles of Leiningen and his unfortunate marriage, while Princess Feodora's eldest son had only recently married a grocer's daughter after various non-matrimonial liaisons. With this family background what might be the future for his own son if left uncurbed?

By the end of November worries over all these events magnified themselves on top of visits to Cambridge, to Sandhurst in pouring rain, and constant sleepless nights. The outbreak of the American Civil War brought the interception of the British *S.S. Trent* on the high seas by a Union warship and the arrest of two Confederate envoys. The Prince toned down a somewhat peremptory British despatch to Washington demanding reparation and leaving President Lincoln's government no avenue of dignified withdrawal. Albert's more conciliatory phrasing expressing the hope that the American captain was not acting under instructions probably averted the outbreak of war, as Lord Palmerston recognized. It was the Prince's last service to England.

The sands were running out. The Prince was tired, sick and exhausted, he lost the will to live. As December progressed, he weakened steadily. He insisted that he had no fever, but typhoid had taken its grip. On 6 December, when the Queen suggested that overwork was the cause of his illness, he agreed. There was a steady decline and on Saturday 14 December he breathed his last at Windsor.

(*opposite*)
Princess Alice, later Grand Duchess of Hesse-Darmstadt (1843–1878)
Engraving by D. J. Pound after a photograph by J. E. Mayall, 1861 (British Museum)

Described by her mother as 'a rarely lovely person', it was perhaps Princess Alice who was best aware of Her father's innermost feelings and to whom the Prince Consort turned for consolation during the last months of his life. Less outwardly brilliant than the Princess Royal, Princess Alice was not only talented but had a much deeper appreciation of the weariness and frustration arising from lack of understanding, even by the Queen, of her father's highly sensitive nature and of the malevolent effect on him of repeated misinterpretation of his actions. She was the mainstay of the Prince during the trying months following the death of the Duchess of Kent, when the Queen gave full vent to prolonged hysterical grief, regardless of its effect on others. Later she gave unstinted help and comfort to the Queen. Alice's task was not easy. The Queen knew too well that her nature was too passionate and her emotions too fervent for the children, however good and loving, to compensate for the loss of a husband who had 'cheered and animated the whole house with his constant good humour and his rare, wonderful mind'.

Princess Alice was already engaged to Prince Louis, afterwards Grand Duke of Hesse-Darmstadt, before Prince Albert's death, and she married him on 1 July 1862. In spite of political upheavals, her marriage was a happy one, cut short by her death from diphtheria, on 14 December 1878. By what the Queen felt to be a curious coincidence Princess Alice was reunited with her father on his very anniversary.

The Tragic Dénouement

Queen Victoria and the Prince Consort
Carte-de-visite, 1861 (Victoria and Albert Museum)

The visiting-card size portrait was made popular in France through Disderi's photographs of Napoleon III. John Edwin Mayall obtained permission to make *carte-de-visite* portraits of all the English Royal Family, resulting in the publication of his *Royal Album* in August 1860. From then on these card photographs became the rage, and portraits not only of the Royal Family, but of other celebrities were on sale at printsellers and stationers. Thousands were sold annually in the early 1860s and exchanged among friends for insertion in albums. They were so popular that on several occasions the government thought of imposing a stamp duty on each photograph, but this idea was abandoned.

(*opposite*)
The Widowed Queen
Engraving by William Holl after a painting by A. Graefle, 1864 (British Museum)

The death of the Prince Consort was a shattering blow to Queen Victoria. Writing to Queen Augusta in September 1863, the Queen exclaimed, 'I cannot describe how sad, desolate and melancholy I feel. My life is without joy, and nothing, nothing can ever bring back one shred of my lost happiness!' However, by 1865 Queen Victoria knew that, although she would 'almost rather sit and weep and live only with Him in spirit and take no interest in the things of this earth', she would have to resume her political and queenly tasks even if she only carried out wearisome things with the thought 'that it is good in his eyes'.

The Prince Consort
Miniature by Edward Moira after a photograph, 1861 (Royal Collection)

128 *The Tragic Dénouement*

The Tragic Dénouement 129

(*opposite*)
The Royal Mausoleum, Frogmore
Watercolour by H. W. Brewer, 1869 (Royal Collection)

Neither the Duchess of Kent nor Prince Albert and Queen Victoria desired to be buried in the royal vaults at Windsor, and a mausoleum had been erected at Frogmore, in Windsor Home Park, for the Queen's mother.

The foundation stone of the Royal Mausoleum was laid by Queen Victoria on 15 March 1862. The style of the building which was based on designs by Ludwig Grüner, worked up by the architect, Albert Jenkins Humbert, was also influenced by the mausoleum at Coburg commissioned by Prince Albert and his brother for their father, Duke Ernest I. On 18 December 1862, the body of Prince Albert was transferred from the entrance to the royal vault in St. George's Chapel, Windsor, to a temporary sarcophagus at Frogmore. The Queen was at the mausoleum. 'Everyone entered, each carrying a wreath. . . We were all much overcome when we knelt round the beloved tomb. When everybody had gone out, we returned again and gazed on the great beauty and peace of the beautiful statue. What a comfort it will be to have that near me!' The coffin was placed in its permanent resting place on 26 November 1868.

The Blue Room at Windsor Castle in which the Prince Consort died in 1861
Photograph (Royal Collection)

The Blue Room into which the Prince Consort was moved the Sunday before his death was the room in which George IV and William IV had both died. A piano was placed in the adjoining room, and there, whilst the other members of the family were at church, Princess Alice, who was in constant attendance on her father during these last fretful days, played his favourite hymn, Luther's *Ein' feste Burg ist unser Gott* (*A Mighty Fortress is our God*).

The Queen was overwhelmed with sadness, referring to 14 December as 'this dreadful, dreadful day!' Writing to the Queen of Prussia from Windsor in November 1864, Queen Victoria declared, 'I love being here and reliving everything in my thoughts! But alas, how desolate it all is. . . Time only makes things emptier and more lonely.'

130 *The Tragic Dénouement*

The Tragic Dénouement 131

The Unveiling of the Prince Consort's Statue in the Market Square at Coburg, 26 August 1865
Watercolour by F. Rothbart (Royal Collection)

On the anniversary of the Prince Consort's birth in 1865 twenty-four members of his family gathered at Coburg for the unveiling of his statue by William Theed in the centre of the Market Square. The Queen had taken up residence at Rosenau on 11 August and was accompanied by all her children except Prince Alfred, in addition to the Princess of Wales, the Crown Prince of Prussia and Prince Louis of Hesse. Duke Ernest II of Coburg stands next to Queen Victoria in this watercolour. At a sign given by him the cover fell from the statue and a loud cheer arose from the dense throng.

132 *The Tragic Dénouement*

Bibliography

Letters of the Prince Consort, 1831–1861. Ed. K. Jagow. London, 1938.

The Prince Consort and his brother. Letters. Ed. H. Bolitho. London, 1933.

The Principal Speeches and Addresses of H.R.H. the Prince Consort. London, 1862.

Queen Victoria's Early Letters, 1821–1861. Ed. J. Raymond. (Revised edition.) London, 1963.

The Letters of Queen Victoria, 1837–1861. Ed. A. C. Benson and Viscount Esher. London, 1908.

Further Letters of Queen Victoria, 1841–1889. Ed. H. Bolitho. London, 1938.

The Letters of Queen Victoria. Second series. A selection from Her Majesty's correspondence and journal, 1862–1878. Ed. G.E. Buckle. London, 1926.

Dearest Child. Letters between Queen Victoria and the Princess Royal, 1858–1861. Ed. R. Fulford. London, 1964.

Dearest Mama. Letters between Queen Victoria and the Crown Princess of Prussia, 1861–1864. Ed. R. Fulford. London, 1968.

The Girlhood of Queen Victoria. A selection of Her Majesty's diaries, 1832–1840. Ed. Viscount Esher. London, 1912.

Victoria travels. Journeys of Queen Victoria between 1830 and 1900, with extracts from her journal. By D. Duff. London, 1970.

Victoria in the Highlands. The personal journal of H.M. Queen Victoria. With notes by D. Duff. London, 1968.

Leaves from a Journal. A record of the visit of the Emperor and Empress of the French to the Queen and of the visit of the Queen and H.R.H. the Prince Consort to the Emperor of the French 1855. With an introduction by R. Mortimer. London, 1961.

Letters of the Empress Frederick. Ed. Sir Frederick Ponsonby. London, 1928.

In Napoleonic Days. Extracts from the private diary of Augusta Duchess of Saxe-Coburg-Saalfeld, 1806–1821. Selected and translated by H.R.H. the Princess Beatrice. London, 1941.

Memoirs of Ernest II. Duke of Saxe-Coburg-Gotha. London, 1888, 1890.

* * *

Albert (Harold A.) *Queen Victoria's sister.* (The life and letters of Princess Feodora.) London, 1967.

Ames (Winslow) *Prince Albert and Victorian Taste.* London, 1967.

Andrews (Keith) *The Nazarenes.* Oxford, 1964.

Ashdown (Dulcie) *Queen Victoria's mother.* London, 1974.

Baedeker (Carl) *Nordwest Deutschland.* Leipzig, 1914.

Balmoral Castle. (Guide.) n.d.

Battiscombe (Georgina) *Queen Alexandra*. London, 1969.

Bauer (Caroline) *Caroline Bauer and the Coburgs*. Ed. C. Nisbet. London, 1885.

Bennett (Daphne) *Vicky, Princess Royal of England and German Empress*. London, 1971.

Bismarck-Schönhausen (Otto von) *Prince*. *Bismarck-Briefe*. Ed. H. Rothfels. Göttingen, 1955.

Bismarck-Schönhausen (Otto von) *Prince*. *Bismarck, reflexions and reminiscences*. London, 1898.

Blunt (Wilfrid) *On Wings of Song. A biography of Felix Mendelssohn*. London, 1974.

Bolitho (Hector) *Albert, Prince Consort*. London, 1964.

Bonn. The University of Bonn. By a member of the Middle Temple. London, 1845.

British Museum. *The Prince Consort, an exhibition*. London, 1961.

Bulman (Joan) *Jenny Lind*. London, 1956.

Bunsen (Frances von) *Baroness*. *A memoir of Baron Bunsen*. London, 1868.

Cecil (*Lord* David) *Lord M*. London, 1954.

Chadwick (George F.) *The Works of Sir Joseph Paxton*. London, 1961.

Charlton (John) *Osborne House*. (Guide.) London, 1974.

Collins-Baker (C. H.) *Catalogue of the principal pictures in the Royal Collection at Windsor Castle*. London, 1937.

Conacher (J. B.) *The Peelites and the Party system, 1846–52*. Newton Abbot, 1972.

Crystal Palace. (A song, beginning 'In Great Hyde Park'.) [London, 1851.]

Cust (*Sir* Lionel H.) *Notes on pictures in the Royal collections*. London, 1911.

D'Auvergne (E. B.) *The Coburgs*. London, 1911.

Descriptive catalogue of a collection of ancient Greek, German, Flemish, etc. pictures, now at Kensington Palace. London, [1848].

Droysen (J. G.) *Carl August and die deutsche Politik*. Jena, 1857.

Duff (David) *Albert & Victoria*. London, 1972.

Eastlake (*Sir* Charles L.) *Contributions to the literature of the Fine Arts.* (Second series.) With a memoir, compiled by Lady Eastlake. London, 1870.

Ebart (Paul von) *Luise Herzogin von Sachsen-Coburg-Saalfeld. Ein Lebensbild nach Briefen derselben*. Minden, 1903.

Eyck (Erich) *Bismarck, Leben und Werk*. Erlenbach-Zürich, 1941–44.

Eyck (Frank) *The Prince Consort, a political biography*. Bath, 1975.

Fleischmann (Adolf) *Zur Geschichte des Herzogthums Sachsen-Coburg*. Hildburghausen, 1880, 1881.

Fox (Caroline) *The Journals of Caroline Fox, 1835–71*. Ed. Wendy Monk. London, 1972.

Fulford (Roger) *The Prince Consort*. London, 1949.

Gash (Norman) *Mr. Secretary Peel*. London, 1961.

Gash (Norman) *Sir Robert Peel*. London, 1972.

Gernsheim (Helmut and Alison) *Queen Victoria*. London, 1959.

Great Exhibition of the Works of Industry of All Nations of 1851. Official descriptive and illustrated catalogue. London, 1851.

Greville (Charles) *The Greville Memoirs*. Ed. R. Fulford. (Revised edition.) London, 1963.

Grey (*Hon.* Charles) *The Early years of H.R.H. the Prince Consort*. London, 1867.

Hardie (Martin) *Water-colour painting in Britain*. London, 1966–68.

Hobhouse (Hermione) *Thomas Cubitt*. London, 1971.

Jameson (Anna B.) *The decorations of the Garden-Pavilion in the grounds of Buckingham Palace, With an introduction by Mrs. Jameson*. London, 1846.

Körner (Hans) *Die Würzburger Siebold. Eine Gelehrten-familie des 18. und 19. Jahrhunderts. Bearbeitet im Auftrage von F. K. von Siebold*. Neustadt a.d. Aisch, 1967.

Levey (Michael) *Painting at Court*. London, 1971.

Longford (Elizabeth) *Victoria R.I.* London, 1964.

Malmesbury, *3rd Earl of. Memoirs of an ex-Minister*. London, 1884.

Maré (Eric de) *London, 1851*. London, 1973.

Martin (*Sir* Theodore) *The Life of H.R.H. the Prince Consort*. London, 1875–80.

Maude (Jenny M. C.) *The Life of Jenny Lind*. London, 1926.

Mendelssohn-Bartholdy (Felix) *Letters*. *Ed*. G. Selden Goth. London, [1946].

Morley (John) *Viscount Morley. The Life of William Ewart Gladstone*. London and New York, 1903.

Noel (Gerard) *Princess Alice*. London, 1974.

Peel (*Sir* Robert) *The Private Letters of Sir Robert Peel*. *Ed*. George Peel. London, 1920.

Ponsonby (D. A.) *The lost Duchess*. London, 1958.

Pound (Reginald) *Albert, a biography of the Prince Consort*. London, 1973.

Reid (*Sir* Thomas W.) *The Life of William Ewart Gladstone*. London, 1899.

Rimmer (Alfred) *The early homes of Prince Albert*. Edinburgh, 1883.

Ringhoffer (C.) *The Bernstorff Papers. The life of Count Albrecht von Bernstorff*. London, 1908.

Rosendahl (Erich) *König Georg V von Hannover*. Hannover, 1928.

Ruland (Carl) *The Works of Raphael, as represented in the Raphael collection in the Royal Library at Windsor Castle, formed by H.R.H. the Prince Consort, 1853–1861, and completed by H.M. Queen Victoria*. [London], 1876.

Saunders (Edith) *A distant Summer*. London, 1947.

Schirmer (Reinhold) *Die städtischen Siedlungen des Obermaingebietes und des Fichtelgebirges*. Erlangen, 1929.

Schultes (Johann A. von) *Sachsen-Koburg-Saalfeldische Landesgeschichte*. Koburg, 1822.

Scott-Elliot (A. H.) *The Etchings by Queen Victoria and Prince Albert*. (Bulletin of the New York Public Library. vol. 65 no. 3. March 1961.)

Stanley (*Lady* Augusta) *Letters of Lady Augusta Stanley, 1849–63*. *Ed*. the Dean of Windsor and H. Bolitho. London, 1927.

Steegman (John) *Consort of taste*. London, 1950.

Stevenson (S. Coles) *Victoria, Albert and Mrs. Stevenson*. [Letters of Mrs. S. C. Stevenson] *Ed*. E. Boykin. London, 1957.

Stockmar (Christian F. von) *Baron. Memoirs of Baron Stockmar. By his son Baron E. Stockmar*. *Ed*. F. Max Müller. London, 1872.

Stoeckl (Agnes de) *King of the French. A portrait of Louis Philippe*. London, 1957.

Talleyrand-Périgord (Dorothée de) *Duchesse de Dino. Memoirs*. *Ed*. the Princess Radziwill. London, 1909, 1910.

Tempeltey (Eduard) *Herzog Ernst von Koburg und das Jahr 1866*. Berlin, 1898.

Valentin (Veit) *the Younger. Fürst Karl Leiningen und das deutsche Einheitsproblem*. Stuttgart, 1910.

Weigall (Rose) *Lady. A Brief Memoir of the Princess Charlotte of Wales*. London, 1874.

Williams (Iolo A.) *Early English Watercolours*. (Reprinted.) Bath, 1970.

Witzleben (Arwied von) *Baron. Prinz Friedrich Josias von Coburg-Saalfeld*. Berlin, 1859.

Woodham-Smith (Cecil) *Queen Victoria*. vol. I. London, 1975.

Woodward (E. L.) *The Age of Reform 1815–1870*. Oxford, 1938.

'How the Christmas tree came to the English Court'. (*The Times*. 22 December 1958.)

* * *

Allgemeine Deutsche Biographie. Leipzig, 1875–1912.

Bénézit (Emmanuel) *Dictionnaire critique et documentaire des peintres*. (Nouvelle édition.) Paris, 1948–55.

Binyon (Robert L.) *Catalogue of drawings by British artists and artists of foreign origin working in Great Britain, preserved in the Department of Prints and Drawings in the British Museum.* London, 1898–1907.

Concise Oxford Dictionary of Opera. By H. Rosenthal and J. Warrack. London, 1964.

Dictionary of National Biography. (Compact edition.) London, 1975.

Grove (*Sir* George) *Grove's Dictionary of Music and Musicians.* (Fourth edition.) London, 1948.

National Gallery. Illustrated General Catalogue. London, 1973.

Neue Deutsche Biographie. Berlin, 1952–

O'Donoghue (F. M.) *Catalogue of engraved British portraits preserved in the Department of Prints and Drawings in the British Museum.* London, 1908–14.

Oxford Companion to Art. Ed. H. Osborne. Oxford, 1970.

Oxford Companion to Music. By Percy A. Scholes. (6th edition.) London, 1945.

Thieme (Ulrich) and Becker (Felix) *Allgemeines Lexikon der bildenden Künstler.* Leipzig, 1907–50.

Wood (Christopher) *Dictionary of Victorian painters.* Woodbridge, Suffolk, [1971.]